PSYCHO-KINESIS

Moving Matter with the Mind

PSYCHO-KINESIS

Moving Matter with the Mind

by

Adrian V. Clark

Parker Publishing Company, Inc.   West Nyack, New York

Reward Edition . . . . . December, 1975
Third Printing . . . . . November, 1976

Library of Congress Cataloging in Publication Data

Clark, Adrian V
Psycho-kinesis.

Includes bibliographical references.
1. Psychokinesis. 2. Psychical research.
I. Title. [DNLM: 1. Parapsychology. BF1171 C592p 1973]
BF1371.C55 133.8'8 73-9782

Printed in the United States of America

Also by the Author:

Cosmic Mysteries of the Universe, 1968, Parker Publishing Company, Inc.

INTRODUCTION

The most demanding desires of the human mind have always been to rise by the "willing of the mind" and soar above the common routine of normal humanity, to obtain fame, fortune, power, friendship, love, and self-satisfaction by controlling the matter around us. This desire has driven men in various directions, with the desire becoming a dream-come-true for many; but yet, the desire continues to be aroused in many more minds as each succeeding generation reaches that level of being aware, that it is possible by the willing of the mind to realize our desires.

Fame by Mind Control

Becoming a millionaire, becoming famous, walking on water, or suddenly being at a new location without being aware of traveling, are experiences recorded in the pages of history, although only a few of these strangely fascinating incidents are acceptable to recognized, prominent historians. These feats of levitation, teleportation, psycho-kinesis, miracles, or being lifted by a spirit, all represent a strange phenomenon which is not understood by the scientific community. Only a very few people have experienced these strange psycho-kinetic occurrences, but many others strive for the key which will unlock the mystery of how to move objects with the mind. Those striving for the secret have generally taken two approaches.

One approach toward becoming famous by moving matter with the mind is the technological approach of developing sufficient knowledge and equipment to be able to move in a vehicle. This was accomplished in a dramatic way by the Wright brothers at Kitty Hawk, and today millions of people have moved through the air in an airplane. The other approach to fame and wealth by controlling our moving has been a study of the mystic, occult forces, which some scholars feel will lead to an easy, cheap way of moving matter. Very few people have moved matter by using this method, but many have moved matter to gain many satisfying benefits for themselves.

Psycho-kinesis is the moving of any object, including one's body, with the mind, by these two methods. One method utilizes improved technology while the other method attempts to use the unknown forces. The utilization of technology for moving objects is the construction and operation of almost any known devices built by man because all of these move objects in the same general way. Obviously the auto moves people from one location to another, but much less obviously, the TV system moves information (pictures and words) from one location to another.

We understand how we move objects using technology and equipment, but we do not understand how we move an object with psychic forces. A better statement would be that someone, not necessarily the one controlling the moving, understands the technology and vehicles, but in psycho-kinesis "someone" may also know how the object is moved. The "someone" in psycho-kinesis may be called a "spirit," "master," "control," etc. In the final analysis, there may be very little difference between moving objects using technology and moving objects using psycho-kinesis. What we learn to help us move matter by conventional means may actually be leading us toward a form of psycho-kinesis, in which we shall understand how the psychic forces function and be able to use them much more effectively.

Mysterious Mind Moves Matter

One of the many unexplainable mysteries of the human mind in this age of technological progress is how the mind can move an object by willing it to move. Although many people may have little interest in determining how the mind performs this feat, they very much want to move an object by thought. At the same time, many others will not accept the possibility of psycho-kinesis since they have never observed it.

Probably one of the best scientific proofs that the mind can control matter was obtained in research conducted by Helmut Schmidt[1] while he was working for the Boeing Company as a Physicist with a PhD degree. He showed that certain people with psychic ability could control the flow of electrons in an electronic system. He performed highly technically controlled scientific tests which proved that psycho-kinesis is a natural phenomenon, although it is not understood. His research will be covered in more detail in Chapter 1. His tests proved that the mysterious human mind, by some preternatural ability, can move the tiny electron so that desired electronic signals could be obtained.

Another well-demonstrated case of psycho-kinesis has been obtained by Jule Eisenbud[2] with Ted Serios, who has the uncanny ability to impose images on photographic film and TV cameras.

In this proof of mind-control-of-matter, Serios moves only extremely small particles, but the result is an intelligible pattern. In tests conducted with Ted Serios by Eisenbud, he was able to control the photons in photographic film and in the vidicon tube in the TV camera to produce an image which came from his mind. He did not know how he accomplished his enigmatic feat, but results were well documented as will be presented in more detail in later chapters.

In addition to Eisenbud's and Schmidt's proofs of psycho-kinesis, there are numerous less well-documented evidences of occult mysteries of the mind. Evidence of psycho-kinesis is told by Mr. Jonsson,[3] the psychic who used ESP to communicate with Ed Mitchell on the *Apollo 13* moon trip. Jonsson claims to be able to

---

[1]Schmidt, Helmut, "New Correlation Between a Human Subject and a Quantum Mechanical Number Generator," No. D1-82-0864, The Boeing Company, Seattle, Washington.

[2]Eisenbud, Jule, *The World of Ted Serios*, William Morrow & Co., Inc., 1967.

[3]Jonsson, *Argosy*, June, 1971, "Can We Really Receive ESP Signals from the Moon?", 205 E. 42nd Street, New York, N.Y.

levitate himself for as much as ten minutes, but is exhausted by the required mental effort. Arthur Ford[4] accepted psycho-kinesis as a natural occult phenomenon. Most students of the occult and religions believe that the human mind has the ability to move objects by thinking about it, but very few people exercise this fantastic ability. With definite proof that psycho-kinesis is possible, more people will try to master this momentous power and many more cases of success will be available. In the scientific community, the researcher will accumulate the data from these cases and, hopefully, determine how psycho-kinesis functions so that it is available to everyone, thus producing a controlled earth environment for the continued existence of future generations. The scientists will develop an understanding of the natural laws which account for psycho-kinesis and use this knowledge to take mankind another step toward the goal of power and happiness.

New Natural Laws

The many occult occurrences are generally considered to be unnatural, supernatural, imaginary, etc., but the occult, if carefully studied and analyzed, can give us an understanding of the natural laws which govern these strange phenomena. Since so much data is already available, the natural laws can be described.

The natural laws for psycho-kinesis would not conflict with already understood ones. Two of the best understood are F=MA or Force equals Mass times Acceleration, and to every action there is an equal and opposite reaction.

It is the understanding of the scientists that any object that moves, must move because it is pushed. To apply this to psycho-kinesis, in which objects are observed to move at the desire of the one with psychic powers, we realize that some force must be moving the object. In the occult language, many names have been applied to this force, such as "odetic," "eloptic," "lovol," ether, etc., but none of these terms are useful to the scientists because they are not associated with known scientific facts. Approaching the question of what psychic force moves the objects, from the

---

[4] Ford, Arthur, *Nothing So Strange,* Harper and Row, Publishers, New York, Evanston, and London, 1958.

scientific facts, we know what force is available to move the objects but not how the force is triggered or controlled.

In order for an object to move itself, it only has to control its molecules so that they push against some surrounding media. As an example, we move our bodies by pushing our feet against the floor, street, etc.—many molecules of the feet are pressing against the floor molecules. Instead of controlling many molecules, as a group, in our feet, if we could control each molecule "independently" and move it against a selected molecule in the floor or air, causing the foot molecules to strike the air molecules with a force, we could walk in the air. Millions of molecules in the feet would strike millions of molecules in the air and lift us as if each moving molecule were a small jet in our feet. But what can control the molecules in the feet to move them individually?

An intelligent being, like the Homo sapiens, moves his molecules by electrical signals from the brain. Some unknown fantastic coding system originates in the brain to generate the electrical signals to move the muscles, hence molecules. At this point we are at the limit of scientific knowledge of how the human brain can signal the movement of molecules without electric signals, as demonstrated by psycho-kinesis. But we know that photons can be the force to move the molecules if we can trigger their release in the desired direction. As the photons leave the molecules, like bullets, the molecules recoil like a gun and thus move. With continued release of photons, as desired, the molecules move as required to strike an air molecule as desired to "lift" the molecules. This action-reaction caused by photon release is known, but very little is known about the signal required to release a photon in a desired direction, and little is known about how to determine the exact position of molecules to understand how they should be moved. Since the unknown natural law concerns how the signal functions, research should be concentrated in this area, and while this is proceeding, there may be another approach to gaining the knowledge of how to move objects.

If an intelligence higher than Homo sapiens exists, and apparently one does, why not ask him how to control psychokinesis? Obviously, the primary reason why not, is that we know no more about how to communicate with higher life than we know about how to move objects with the mind. Based upon considerable evidence, practice and experimentation may be more important in establishing a reliable contact with higher life than knowing the natural laws and how to control psychic forces.

Violation of Force Equals Mass Times Acceleration

Among the students of the occult, religion, and related non-scientific areas, many people feel that known natural laws are set aside for psycho-kinesis, faith-healing, miracles, etc. Such an idea is based primarily upon a lack of understanding of natural laws, which are the rules by which nature functions. Therefore, if known natural laws were set aside, this idea would become a natural law in itself, because it would be a rule by which nature functions. But this has not been observed in nature. It seems more probable that all occult, religious, and strange phenomena come under the rules already understood plus some natural laws not yet known.

Specifically, psycho-kinesis probably obeys the law dictating that the moving of an object requires a force. In the occult language, this force is nebulously called psychic, "odetic," etc., without understanding that the force is a result of a physical object reacting with the object being moved. In psycho-kinesis, the force which does the moving is as real as the man who lifts a child, but the psychic force may be much more difficult to detect than a man. It is very unlikely that psycho-kinesis violates the natural law of F=MA, and in trying to detect the psychic force, we should assume that all known natural laws will remain valid.

An Easy Way to Travel or Move Furniture

In our efforts to gain the great potential of teleportation, we may have little desire to understand how psycho-kinesis functions, but our primary desire may be to use it for a major task, such as traveling to other planets or a minor effort like moving furniture. However, if psycho-kinesis is similar to other natural phenomena, someone will have to understand how it functions before we can construct equipment and instruct others in how to operate the equipment. As an example familiar to all of us, most people do not know how electricity performs its many functions, but any child can flip the switch to turn on lights, start motors, move vehicles, etc. For the child to be able to do so much with electricity, someone had to learn how electricity functioned and construct equipment to utilize it. In a similar manner, to utilize psycho-kinesis, someone may have to understand it through research, and develop equipment, techniques, etc. for others to use. It is only when enough people are researching, trying new ideas, and testing that data is obtained.

Gaining fame, moving of furniture, or traveling may be easy if we understand psycho-kinesis or can use it, but we may cause problems if it is used with insufficient understanding of how it works.

The Controls May Be Stringent

In all natural phenomena, there are rules and regulations. Nature has a set of rules for us to follow to be successful. Therefore, nature dictates that the use of psycho-kinesis will entail obeying the rules which may be by far the tightest controls imposed upon any of the many natural, powerful forces available for our use. As we are well aware, the natural laws used in the simple moving of objects are learned as a normal part of every youth's education.

The normal baby learns to move his hands and discovers that certain movements, such as hitting his face, can hurt him. He learns to crawl and discovers that he must direct his crawling or run into unpleasant obstacles. He begins to ride a tricycle and skins his hands and knees while learning that speed must be controlled. He learns to drive a car and must know the driving regulations to pass his driver's test and avoid accidents. He can learn to fly a plane and must obey a much more stringent set of rules in handling his moving object, the airplane. And a few men have learned to control a space vehicle for a trip to the moon and a return to earth. These astronauts have spent years learning the many stringent rules which must be obeyed if they are to move an object, themselves and their vehicle, to the moon and back safely.

There are many indications that the field of psycho-kinesis will have even more stringent rules for its use than rules for going to the moon. Yet, the basic principles will be the same; i.e., conserve energy and do not harm yourself or others. Since these basic principles are already being followed by most people, the primary area of research should be how to use psycho-kinesis.

Success by Trial

From the beginning of recorded history, mankind has used the mysterious psycho-kinesis without knowing how it works; and for an even longer time has used oxygen without knowing, until recently, that it even existed. Therefore, with continued efforts and more scientific controls being applied as data is obtained, psycho-kinesis can become as thoroughly understood and commonly used as oxygen (which is now used for many purposes other than breathing). Each person who develops the ability to control, to any extent, the powerful, awesome force that moves objects with the mind can tell us how to use psycho-kinesis more easily. By trying to use our psychic powers, many of us may receive a few rewards while some will be highly successful. With each attempt to use this awesome force, more data can be gained, and if each person will send their information to this author or other scientists working in the psychic field (Astronaut Ed Mitchell, Helmut Schmidt, Jim Beal, etc.), the data can be analyzed and progress made in the psychic field.

As has been demonstrated by the moon trips, when enough people are convinced that a task is possible and enough people work on the task, it is accomplished; therefore, with many people convinced of psycho-kinesis, which they will be if they will try the techniques proposed in this book, psycho-kinesis may become as common as the use of electricity.

How to Be Convinced

To be convinced that psycho-kinesis is possible and try to move an object with the mind will be difficult for some individuals, while others will be easily convinced. To be convinced that we can move an object with our minds is comparable to being convinced that God exists, that UFO's are real, or that we have a sixth sense. Usually we must have some strong experiences affecting our five senses to be convinced that some nebulous phenomenon is real.

Arthur Ford[5] was convinced of psychic powers, including telekinesis. He told how Mrs. St. Clair Stobart, an outstanding researcher in English spiritualism, became convinced of telekinesis and began her impressive career in the psychic field.

Shortly after World War I, Mrs. Stobart received a request from a Western Canadian friend asking her to arrange a sitting for a friend by proxy. Although Mrs. Stobart had no interest in the psychic field, she went to the best place she knew about, the British College of Psychic Science, and had a sitting with a tested medium. She obtained a transcript of the sitting which she sent to her Canadian friend, who wrote back verifying the information the British medium had obtained. This aroused Mrs. Stobart's interest which caused her to attend a series of experiments being conducted by the College of Psychic Science with Frau Silbert of Graz, Austria. In the experiment, Mrs. Stobart saw many demonstrations of telekinetic and other enigmatic powers of Silbert and was convinced that psychic powers were real and available. As more and more people, like Mrs. Stobart, are convinced that psycho-kinesis is possible, they will obtain results which can be analyzed to improve on techniques and accumulation of data.

If we can be convinced that psycho-kinesis is possible, it will become a reality–and another of mankind's dreams will come true.

Adrian V. Clark

---

[5]Ford, Arthur, *Nothing So Strange*, Harper and Row, Publishers, New York, Evanston, and London, 1958.

ACKNOWLEDGMENTS

This book has been contributed to by many friends and interested persons. I wish, gratefully, to acknowledge their valuable assistance in supplying information contained herein.

I also acknowledge the contribution in critical analysis and thoughts provided by my wife and life's partner. She has been a great stabilizing influence on my imagination, pulling me back to practical reality.

The person who has contributed most intensively of her time and thoughts is Flo Lyles, who prepared and edited the many reworks of the manuscript. She also contributed ideas, concepts, and theories which are a part of this work in a young, challenging area of science.

A.V.C.

TABLE OF CONTENTS

1. MOVING OBJECTS WITH THE MIND

At first glance, moving objects by "thinking of moving them" may seem very far from reality; however, a close examination of how the human race has accomplished a tremendous moving job already, and how it may not be far from being able to move planets, will demonstrate that moving objects with the mind is what we are accomplishing.

All Movement May Be by Mind Control

In the technological field, many discoveries have been made because the scientists, or laymen, with curiosity, have been willing to investigate open-mindedly a seemingly ridiculous area. Electric lights, airplanes, T.V., radio, autos, household appliances, and many other inventions fall into this category, although people have become conditioned to discoveries and new developments and they are not as skeptical as they were before this modern technological era.

Even though we are more open minded about new ideas and discoveries, we continue to be reluctant to try moving an object with our mind because this seems to be completely unassociated with known data. We have not reviewed the data available on the subject and drawn our conclusions from the facts. As we review the data of psycho-kinesis (P-K), if we use a broad definition of P-K, we shall realize that all movement is psycho-kinesis.

Whether we move ourselves with our muscles or speed to the moon in a space vehicle, we move because thoughts have been converted into action which causes the vehicle to move from one location to another. As an example, we move an airplane from New York to Los Angeles because thoughts of how to design, construct, and operate the airplane have gone into its movements. In addition, thoughts are continually directing and controlling the aircraft on the trip from New York to Los Angeles. We may consider the moving of the aircraft to be by its engines, but these would not move the aircraft if the engines were not designed in the proper manner. Even the fuel consumed by the engines is a product of mankind's ingenuity, hence a result of thoughts.

As a result of mankind's quest for knowledge, we have learned a lot about moving objects and how to control their movement. Although we control the movement of our muscles, legs, arms, tricycles, roller skates, bicycles, motorcycles, automobiles, trains, boats, airplanes, space vehicles, etc., there are many other objects which we have observed to be moving, over which we have no control, nor do we understand what causes them to move.

The earth moves by rotating while circling the sun, which also moves through space. The earth is not unique in its behavior because the astronomers tell us that billions of suns in the universe exhibit the same behavior as our sun in this solar system, and the earth's movement has been attributed to gravity, inertia, solar system formation, the "big bang," and other natural laws and theories. Yet we do not fully understand what causes the earth to move or what started it moving; in fact, it took a genius like Einstein to have much understanding of moving objects, and he admitted that there was much he didn't understand.

Einstein defined all motion as relative; i.e., no object moves except as measured from some other object. He would say that for a person standing on the earth, it does not move with respect to that person, but with respect to the sun, other planets, stars, etc. When a person walks, Einstein would say that he moved with respect to an observer who was standing still, but if the observer were moving with the walker, Einstein could define the earth as moving with respect to the observer. This gives a peculiar picture of a man walking on an 8,000-mile diameter ball with the man stationary and the ball revolving beneath his feet like a giant treadmill. Einstein may have even considered the mental leap to the question of "whether the man was moving himself, by thought, or was moving the entire earth by thought converted into muscle action?" With this mental approach, a type of P-K is being exercised to move the earth, but let's consider much smaller objects which are moving.

With highly refined, sophisticated equipment, the scientist has been able to detect (see) extremely small objects down to the sub-particles in the nucleus of an atom. He has found that all objects detected to date have been moving with respect to him. So far he has concluded that all objects have a motion, and he has found that some particles such as the photons, or light particles, do not exist at any velocity less than 186,000 miles per second! Other particles also demonstrate this strange phenomenon that the scientists call "zero rest mass." Although some particles may not seem to exist at rest, they theoretically could, but not be detectable, because all known detection equipment operates on the principle that a force must be exerted on the instrument before it detects the object which exerts the force. And an object at rest with respect to the detecting instrument cannot exert a force on it.

With our present understanding of natural laws, we must conclude that an object which does not move, does not exist.

Let us take an imaginary trip on a photon traveling at 186,000 miles per second and observe the view around us. According to Einstein's theory, we shall observe that all motion has stopped; the entire universe as we pass through it will be completely stationary—a still picture. But it is only by imagination that we could travel at 186,000 miles per second or be able to see stationary objects. If we restrict our imagination to traveling at 186,000 miles per second, but having to detect the universe with the usual scientific equipment (telescopes, radar, etc.), we would not "see" anything since everything would be still and we would exist in a void. These imaginary excursions illustrate how, with our vast knowledge of our universe, we have inconsistencies in our theories; hence, the theories are not yet established natural laws.

Since nothing exists by our methods of detection unless it is moving, who or what caused the initial motion and what is the driving force to continue the motion? Since we have no definite answer to the question, even if it is a valid question, we have satisfied ourselves to some degree with the indeterminate answer that "God" is the driving force or source of energy. In the scientific realm, the closest answer to the energy source is photon energy, which originates in stars from thermonuclear reaction of hydrogen which is found throughout space, and the source of hydrogen is possibly photon energy, thus completing a cycle which still doesn't answer the question of the source of energy for moving objects. If we say that a psychic force or spiritual force moves all matter, we are still not answering the question unless we can define the force. Since the force has not been defined, to say that God is the moving force is as good an answer as any, yet it is still not an answer.

The force to move objects is available as photon energy, and the prime question to accomplish the awesome psycho-kinesis is to learn how to control the forces available. This question is typical of many facing the research scientist–i.e., how to control a known energy source–and he has learned how to control energy in many different ways.

But the inherent ambition of man to move, travel, create, easier and easier, drives him on to shorten the steps from the thoughts to the moving of the objects. We have instant T.V. at the flip of a switch, instant foods by adding water and heating, instant playback on T.V., and many other instant commodities–and we continue to seek instant travel, instant money, instant happiness, etc.

Shortening the Steps from Thought to Movement

The thought that I want to move myself from my home to Los Angeles, results in my moving several thousand miles. If I did not have the "thought," I would not have moved. (In some cases another person could have the thought which moved me.) Of course there is some lapse of time from the "thought" to the "moving," but there is much less time involved in the moving time today than there was 200 years ago. With our modern means of transportation, the time from thought to arrival is about five hours–but 200 years ago, the trip would have required several months. With scientific progress, we have considerably shortened the time from thought to arrival, but we want a faster, cheaper system that will move us effortlessly at no cost from here to Los Angeles.

There is no doubt that the time required to move from one location to another can be shortened, but faster travel always costs more money, yet more people have more money and more people can pay the price to travel faster. The shortest possible travel time for moving would be near the photon velocity according to scientific theories, but travel involving people has not begun to approach 186,000 miles per second. The space vehicle reaches a maximum of about 35,000 feet per second, which is presently the maximum speed attained by human beings, but this high velocity is almost nothing compared to the velocity of light.

If P-K will enable us to take a giant leap from the "slow" space vehicle velocity to the faster-than-light psychic velocity, there will be many new concepts in the scientific fields. One concept which may be drastically changed is our concept of time, or the measure of the sequence of events. The concept of time is closely related to human beings, their rate of motion, thinking rates, and life span. If we were not limited in life span, would we be time conscious? If we were not time conscious, would we have made so much progress in the technological realm? Since we have made much progress in faster methods of travel, we will undoubtedly discover much faster methods of traveling, and P-K seems to be the fastest method of travel "known." Although very little is known about P-K, there is sufficient knowledge in this challenging field to indicate that a major breakthrough is close.

The psychic realm may hold the key to the powerful P-K forces which can give us instantaneous travel to anywhere in the universe. Not travel of one object (our body) from one planet to another, but some mysterious relocation of ourselves by dissolving the body at the departure point and reconstructing it at the destination. The key may not be discovery of how to propel ourselves at faster and faster speeds, but how to traverse from this physical system to the psychic system or Unobstructed Universe,[1] and return back to a precise location in the physical world. If the key is found to unlock the door to the spirit realm and return to the physical, the traveling time may be shortened to no time from the thought to the arrival at the desired location. Where short trips are desired or the moving of objects over short distances is the goal, another type of P-K may move the object directly under thought control.

Will the Force Still Equal Mass Times Acceleration?

Considering the direct method of moving an object with the mind, such as lifting a pencil off the desk top, will the mysterious forces that move the pencil and the pencil's movement obey the natural laws such as F = MA (where F is force used to move an object with mass M at an acceleration A), since in all cases where objects move, such as automobiles, airplanes, etc., which have been scientifically investigated, the natural law of F = MA has been valid? In the psychic realm, not many, if any, cases have been investigated, but based upon the observed consistency in nature, when the psychic forces can be detected, the law of F = MA will probably hold, although there can be further refinement of the equation as has occurred many times in our technological advancement.

As an example of where F = MA is not directly applicable is in the movement of photons which never accelerate or decelerate like other physical objects, but the photon, if it exists, is traveling at 186,000 miles per second without an acceleration period. In the psychic universe, all supernormal material may be following a behavior pattern which does not find applications in natural laws of the physical universe. However, when an object is moved by psychic forces and it remains in the physical universe, the mysterious forces moving the object will probably fit the natural law of F = MA. There will probably be a psychic triggering activity which then utilizes the physical material for the movement of the object. In P-K the psychic forces may trigger the release of

---

[1] White, Stewart, *The Unobstructed Universe,* E.P. Dutton & Co., New York, 1940.

photons in air molecules, which cause the air molecules to lift the object and move it. This fascinating possibility will be explained in following chapters.

Control of the Alpha Rhythm Brain Wave by Unknown Methods

The alpha rhythm brain wave is associated with ESP by some researchers,[2] and it has been controlled in frequency and amplitude by certain people. This brain wave is detected with standard electroencephalograph (EEG) equipment when the brain is relaxed, but alert, prior to dozing or going to sleep. The brain wave has a normal frequency of 8-16 cycles per second, which has been associated with ESP ability in many test cases. If the alpha rhythm brain wave is strong, the ESP is better.

In special experiments, subjects have been connected to an EEG with their brain wave on display on an oscilloscope. They have been asked to vary their strange brain wave in amplitude and frequency. Without any concept of how they control this wave, the subjects have been successful in controlling it.

With a crude understanding of brain physiology, it can be stated that the subject controls electrical signals in his head, which is what he does while thinking or performing any other conscious brain functions. In the same way that we do not know how we think or control our muscles with our brain, the subject does not know how he controls the alpha rhythm brain wave. Since he controls electrical signals in his brain, he is also controlling the emission of photons in his brain, because electrical energy produces photons and photons can produce electrical signals.

Since the brain has the ability to control the emission of photons within itself, with special training the brain may be able to control the emission of photons outside itself, and P-K would be possible through known techniques.

Some very interesting scientific research using the alpha rhythm brain wave, associated with ESP, has been conducted by Drs. T.D. Duane and Thomas Behrendt[3] of Jefferson Medical

---

[2]Rhine, Joseph D., *New Frontiers of the Mind,* Holt, Rinehart, and Winston, Inc., New York, 1937.

[3]*Huntsville Times,* January 19, 1966.

College, Philadelphia. Their research has caused many scientists to take a more serious look at extrasensory perception (ESP). This research involves the alpha rhythm brain wave which is the wave pattern that is characteristic of a person who is sitting quietly with his eyes closed and his mind at ease. This condition is the meditation state utilized by some people to contact the spirit world. Other mental conditions also have characteristic trademarks which can be recognized from the brain wave patterns. We experience many mental states such as anger, fear, dreaming, alertness, etc., all of which produce definite brain wave patterns.

Identical twins seemed to be able to induce alpha rhythm in each other by extrasensory means better than other people. They were seated about 15 feet apart in separate rooms. Each twin had installed on his head electrodes which picked up his brain waves. In testing the twins, one was told to close his eyes in order to produce the characteristic alpha rhythm brain waves. The brain wave patterns were monitored on both twins.

The researchers have found that about two out of 15 pairs of twins have been able to induce brain waves in their twin. When one twin closed his eyes while the other twin kept his eyes open, the twin with his eyes open had the characteristic alpha rhythm brain wave. The researchers called this phenomenon "extrasensory induction of brain waves between individuals who are separated." These experimenters have also conducted tests with unrelated persons, but they did not note the appearance of any alpha rhythm in the second person when it was evoked in the first. Researchers in parapsychology at Duke University traditionally have used decks of cards to determine the ESP ability of subjects. The researchers have found that those people who score high on these tests have a higher degree of alpha rhythm. As the subject improves his score, the alpha rhythm strength also increases, or there is a greater abundance of the alpha rhythm signals. From these indications, it appears that a relaxed attitude of the conscious mind, or low mental activity, produces a stronger ESP ability.

There is a relationship between a relaxed mind and a drowsy mind. When the mind becomes drowsy, the person's ESP ability decreases. Researchers Duane and Behrendt also conducted tests with two persons where one was sleeping throughout the night and the other person, 400 feet away, studied reproductions of great paintings. Results of this testing showed a close connection between the nature of paintings and the contents of dreams of the person who was asleep.

Mrs. Thelma Moss,[4] a graduate psychologist of UCLA, has conducted another type of experiment between two persons which gives substantiating evidence of telepathic signals. In her experiment, two people, one a transmitter and the other a receiver, were placed in separate rooms where they could neither see nor hear one another. The person called the transmitter was then exposed to various emotional stimuli which were calculated to evoke various strong reactions. At the same time, the environment of the receiver was quiet and undisturbed, placing him in a relaxed condition. The emotional states were produced by showing the transmitter various pictures which would cause an emotional reaction. In addition he was given physical stimuli, such as placing his feet in ice water, and one of the most emotional reactions was produced by showing a series of slides which recorded President John F. Kennedy's assassination.

After evoking each emotional state, the one who was stimulated through his senses was asked to state his emotional reactions to those things which he saw and heard. Completely separate from him, the receiver was also asked to tell what was on his mind at that time, although he neither saw nor heard any of the things that were happening to the transmitter in the adjoining room. Testing was conducted with some 30 experimental teams. In addition, there were ten others who acted as a control group. The ten who were the control group were placed in a room and told to relax and give their impressions of what was happening to the person in the next room, yet there was no one in the adjoining room.

The testing showed that when sensations of cold and discomfort were transmitted, 56% of the receivers reported that they had experienced some discomfort of being cold. Not a single one of the control groups reported anything of this type. A description of a Hawaiian Island, water, waves, etc. caused 83% of the real receivers and only 33% of the controlled group to report similar thoughts. The most significant indication of ESP was that, according to Mrs. Moss, the only proper name mentioned during the testing by the receivers was that of President Kennedy. He was

---

[4] *The Huntsville Times*, January 19, 1966.

mentioned five times by five different receivers, but none of the control group mentioned his name. These tests showed that some unknown signal, which may be the key to moving matter, passed from the transmitter to the receiver.

Gifted Brains Control Electrons

Very conclusive results of controlled experiments by highly qualified researchers have shown that some psychics are able to control the movement of electrons, which is that part of the atom orbiting the nucleus. The electron is the source of the photons. The results of experiments by Schmidt,[5] Eisenbud[6], and others demonstrate that some gifted individuals can control the activity of electrons, and since they move electrons, P-K has been proven on a small scale.

The research conducted by Helmut Schmidt, a physicist with the Boeing Co., Seattle, Washington, was begun because of Schmidt's natural curiosity about laboratory experiments being influenced by the experimenter. He suspected that an observed physical phenomenon, quantum jump, was triggered by the experimenter. Since he could not directly measure a person's ability to cause a jump and the results, he developed an electronic device, a random number generator using a classical flip-flop circuit.

The device had on the exterior four lights, with a button near each light. When a button was depressed, one of the four lights would come on. After controlled tests, the device was verified to be truly random, with the probability that any one of the lights would turn on 25% of the time. When a button was pressed, the chances that the light near the button would light was one in four. The device also had an internal recorder of which button was pressed and which light came on.

After the device had been thoroughly tested, Schmidt selected several subjects and tested their ability to control the device. He found that most people have some influence on the device, but those with artistic talents obtained the best results. He also tested several people who claimed to have psychic abilities, and three of them experienced phenomenal results with the machine. He had

---

[5]Schmidt, Helmut, "New Correlation Between a Human Subject and a Quantum Mechanical Random Number Generator," The Boeing Company, 1967.

[6]Eisenbud, Jule; *The World of Ted Serios,* William Morrow and Co., Inc., 1967.

the three psychics conducting tests at various times and places until they had accumulated over 30,000 tries.

The three psychics racked up an unbelievable score, showing that they did truly influence the device. They had accomplished a feat which had a statistical probability of one in a billion. Statistically speaking, 1 billion tests would have to be conducted of over 30,000 tries each, before, on a random basis, the score which had been achieved by the psychics would be repeated. The three psychics undoubtedly influenced the functioning of the flip-flop circuit, the tape recorder, or unknown facts, any one of which was a demonstrated evidence of psycho-kinesis in the form of moving electrons outside the brain. And if these three psychics could move the extremely small electron with brain activity, we also may be able to move larger objects by practice and a better understanding of how an object is moved by P-K.

Dr. Schmidt was so impressed by the results, that he tried to publish the data in various technical journals, but without success, since most technical journals do not recognize parapsychology as an area of science. However, Dr. Schmidt, rather than being discouraged, left the Boeing Co. to work with Dr. Rhine at the Institute of Parapsychology in Durham, N.C., where he is continuing research which could lead to a major discovery of our time. But there is also the possibility that he and other researchers are so far from understanding P-K that a breakthrough may be far away.

In the meantime, since we know that P-K is possible, we can use this psychic phenomenon by following development techniques which have been successfully used by others. We can find many famous psychics who will tell us how to improve our psychic power, but all methods seem to require much effort and time to master. Most of us are looking for a simple, effortless method of controlling matter, like turning on the T.V. It may be through research that this method of utilizing the psychic forces will be realized. Some people may not feel that it's worth the time and effort to become psychic through development of our natural occult capabilities, but they would use a machine to perform a task by control of spiritual energy.

A Mind Moves Film Emulsion

Some psychics developed their special abilities, while others were born with a gift which they do not understand. Some psychics have high moral values, while others have low moral standards. There seems to be little, if any, correlation between morality and psychic ability, except that most psychics attach a religious significance to their occult powers.

A very strangely gifted psychic who has baffled the scientific institutes is Ted Serios,[7] who does not attach any religious significance to his special odd talent. During tests being conducted at the University of Colorado, Serios was in and out of all sorts of scrapes in bars, he was jailed, and he was beaten up in drunken brawls. In spite of Serios' lack of moral restraints, he was able to perform many paranormal feats for Dr. Eisenbud and other researchers. He specialized in imposing mental images on photographic film! However, like all psychics, he displayed strong occult powers at some times while having no psychic abilities at others.

At the beginning of Eisenbud's work with Serios, on the first day of testing, it was late in the evening after a fruitless day of photography that the first proof of Serios' fantastic paranormal ability was obtained. The method of testing was Serios' choice and consisted of taking a picture of a "gismo" such as a plastic cylinder, about a half-inch in diameter and a half-inch high, one end being covered with plain cellophane and the other end covered with cellophane over a piece of film darkened by stove black. Although the researchers were suspicious of the gismo, they could determine no way that it could be some trick device. When the picture was taken, the gismo would be so close to the camera that it would be out of focus. The first successful result was what appeared to be a blurred image of Westminster Abbey.

After this initial success, many other paranormal photographs were obtained, some with such detail that letters could be seen in the photograph. Probably the best example was the imposed image of Williams' Livery stable in Central City, Colorado which showed the word "Livery" over a doorway. When the paranormal photo was compared to one taken a few days later of the actual building, they were very similar, even to the extent that a shadow cast by a wall lantern was in the same location on both photos!

Being suspicious that the entire Ted Serios story could be a fraud, I had some of the photos examined by a photographic expert, who explained that some of the paranormal photos were possibly trick photography, but he was very puzzled by some

---

[7] Eisenbud, Jule, *The World of Ted Serios,* William Morrow and Company, Inc., 1967.

things in the paranormal photos which were different from the actual pictures.

I continued the investigation by contacting a friend who had visited with Dr. Eisenbud, and I was assured by the friend that the entire story was legitimate. I then called Dr. Eisenbud and discussed his ideas about how Serios was able to accomplish his special occult feat.

Eisenbud considers the Serios phenomenon to be a special P-K ability. He theorizes that Serios makes contact with universal consciousness, who, through Serios' brain, controls the release of photons in a pattern in the film emulsion.

The unusual Ted Serios might have imposed images on film with a communication link to the universal intelligence. His speciality, when in contact with the universal intelligence, was to cause a chemical reaction in the film in the camera. The chemical reaction was probably produced by the emission of light which exposed the film. The pattern of exposure was a result of Serios producing a psychic signal which, when linked with the universal intelligence, had sufficient control of power to release photons systematically from the area of the emulsion to produce the desired image on the film.

When light falls on the film, a chemical reaction is produced. This chemical reaction turns silver into a black silver compound; therefore, the portions of the film which receive most light are darkest. Possibly Ted Serios had the psychic ability to communicate with the universal mind and tap the powers available there to control intellectually the release of photons from the camera film emulsion in a desired pattern.

The research conducted by Schmidt and Eisenbud produced convincing data that P-K is a natural phenomenon within the realm of scientific investigation. The research is continuing, and it may soon lead to production of equipment which will allow the powerful P-K forces to be available to everyone; however, P-K can already be commanded by almost anyone who will follow the training techniques which were established by the experts in the psycho-kinesis field.

Psycho-Kinetic Surgery

Actual movie film is available at the Psychic Research Foundation, Chicago, Illinois of psycho-kinetic surgery being performed by a man in the Philippines. This film has been shown on a television program entitled, "News of the Psychic World." In addition to the film, a book by Harold Sherman, *Wonder Healers of the Philippines,* tells how men are performing astounding major operations with their bare hands, without equipment or antiseptics, utilizing a unique, new form of psycho-kinetics for the potential benefit of all mankind.

The Philippino man in the movie considers his ability to have been obtained from God and he will not charge for the surgery, although he will accept donations. When he performs the operation, he selects the area for an incision. Then he separates the flesh as if it were being cut, but he uses only his hands and mind, which is apparently linked to the superintelligence. He is apparently separating flesh by controlling the release of photons in the molecules of the flesh, which can break down chemical bonds, and the flesh separates as if he sliced it with a scalpel.

As the flesh separates, there is no blood or fluids. The psycho-kinetic surgeon corrects the defective organ with his hands only, even though there may be more cutting and reconnecting required. Then he closes the incision without stitches or clamps.

At the completion of the operation, the incision does not show–no scar–nor does the patient have any soreness. He is immediately completely recovered from the operation as if it had not been performed at all, as if he had been faith healed. During the operation, the patient feels nothing, even though he is wide awake without even local anesthetic.

In the movie, which showed both an eye operation and a stomach operation, the patient showed no signs of pain or unpleasant sensations during the entire operation. When it was completed, he walked away completely healed by psycho-kinetic surgery, performed by a man who had followed the technique of having confidence in a superior intelligence to allow him to exercise tremendous psychic powers.

Confidence

In ESP research,[8] it has been determined that those people who express optimism in performing ESP tests obtain a higher

---

[8]"ESP Accepted as a Field of Science," *Huntsville Times,* Aug. 22, 1971.

score than those who lack confidence. Therefore, it would seem that faith produces positive results for the optimist, even if it is just faith in his own ability.

With an extra-terrestrial being telling us what is needed to move a mountain and ESP researchers telling us that faith improves ESP, we should be improving our faith in order to move mountains. We may find that the primary obstacle to P-K is developing confidence that we can move objects with our minds.

As an interesting story, rather than evidence of how to move objects with the mind, I asked a medium who was being controlled by a being on Jupiter how this extra-terrestrial being traveled. His reply was that he converted everything for the trip into anti-matter, except the identity particle. Having examined his answer, I concluded that he meant that he traveled by thought; i.e., being at a new location by having detailed knowledge that he was at the new location.

After many years of investigating psychic phenomena, I have found that many gimmicks, gismos, machines, etc. are being used by psychics who claim that the device has some special occult function; however, I suspect that all such devices are aids to develop confidence, and if they develop confidence that we can communicate with higher powers, the device works because our faith becomes stronger.

Obtain Yes or No Answers by Movement of Objects

In the world of the occult, there are many techniques for obtaining yes or no answers by the movement of an object or objects which are supposedly controlled by psychic powers. Some of the techniques are Ouija Boards, pendulums, forked sticks or rods for water witching, turning of a straw on a ripe melon, movements of our body, tilting of a table, and others. All such techniques require that the one asking the questions be in contact with the object which moves to give the answer. In a few cases, these techniques have been observed to give excellent results. Usually this is true when the user has confidence, or faith, but the techniques fail when the user lacks confidence.

The movement of objects under the controls of the user (although he does not consciously control them) seems to be a special type of psycho-kinesis. The movement is probably caused by involuntary muscle action initiated by the subconscious mind, and the subconscious mind may have responded to a psychic signal from the universal energy intelligence.

When we request an answer by movement of an object held in our hand, we assume that the psychic powers know the answer and will move us and the object. When we request that an object be moved which is not held in our hand, we assume that we know where the object should move but we don't have the power to move the object. As we will an object at a distance to move, psychic forces not understood by the commander must move the object. When we ask a question and the object in our hand moves, we understand the forces (muscular) moving the object, but we don't have knowledge of how or which way the object should move to give the correct answer.

The obtaining of yes or no answers as an object is moved in our hand is a start toward control of P-K at a distance, because the yes-no answer methods give us confidence to try more difficult tasks.

Moving of objects with the mind is not only a fascinating possibility but also has been accomplished by selected individuals. When examined in its broadest sense, P-K may be applied to all movement since all activity may be controlled by a super-intelligence. What is desired by most of us is a short-cut to going places faster with little effort on our part, which seems selfish but may be acceptable to the super-intelligence if his laws are not violated. Psycho-kinesis has been checked and proven in scientific tests, which places it on a firmer footing with scientists, even though P-K was used by ancient seers and was explained by extra-terrestrial beings thousands of years ago. As we acquire the history of psycho-kinesis, we can perform miraculous feats through increased confidence.

A Fast Buck by Mind Power

On a triumphant evening in Germany in 1958, three happy young American service men had successfully completed a difficult assignment. To celebrate, they were at an officer's club, drinking, gambling, and enjoying their elation in having completed their task. One of the men, now an engineer with NASA, and a friend of the writer, related this story.

As they played the slot machines in the club, they had confidence that they could control the machines to make them pay off. They began playing nickel machines, but worked up to quarter machines as their confidence was reconfirmed with jackpots. They were rewarded with wins until they had cleaned out about five of the slot machines. Because they had confidence in their psycho-kinetic ability, they obtained money from the machines.

Although the NASA engineer who told me the story feels that he can still control slot machines, which he did one other time in Las Vegas, he does not recommend using psychokinesis to gain wealth. He feels that psycho-kinesis should be used to help other people, which would benefit both the one controlling psycho-kinesis and the person who is helped.

Negative Attitudes Impede Progress

One of the best-documented cases of outstanding psychokinetic ability is that of Neyla Mikhailova[9], Leningrad, Russia. Her unbelievable feats of moving objects by mental effort alone have been subjected to many scientific tests. These feats are recorded not only in scientific reports and journals, but in motion pictures as well.

Neyla Mikhailova had some very difficult times in her younger days. As a front line soldier against the Germans in the battle for Leningrad, at the age of 15, she rose to the rank of sergeant before wounds ended her army career. Today she is a typical Russian housewife, the wife of an engineer and the mother of one son whom she feels has inherited her psycho-kinetic ability, just as she feels that she inherited her talents from her mother.

Neyla's first awareness of her psycho-kinetic abilities came while she was recovering from an illness in a Leningrad hospital. Occupying her time with embroidery, she had by her bed a large bag of various-colored embroidery thread. Without glancing into the bag, she was able to draw out the exact color thread that she needed for the work she was doing. She had seen an article in a newspaper about Rosa Kuleshova, who claimed to be able to see

[9] Ostrander, Sheila and Schroeder, Lynn, *Psychic Discoveries Behind the Iron Curtain,* Bantam Books, Prentice-Hall, Inc., Englewood Cliffs, New Jersey, 1970.

colors with her hands. This encouraged Mrs. Mikhailova to report her own strange ability to her doctors.

When the news of her uncanny abilities later came to the attention of Dr. Loenid Vasiliev, one of Russia's greatest physiologists, he investigated by subjecting her to many carefully controlled laboratory tests. Dr. Vasiliev theorized that some form of energy may flow from her hands to enable her to "see" the colors. Remembering tests conducted by a Greek researcher, Dr. Vasiliev obtained a compass and asked Neyla to pass her hands above it. Because the needle turned, he considered her to have definite psycho-kinetic abilities.

Mrs. Mikhailova has experienced moments of spontaneous psycho-kinesis as well as those intentional conscious efforts at psycho-kinesis when laboratory tests were being conducted. Several years ago as she was approaching a cabinet while in a very angry and tense mood, a pitcher suddenly moved to the edge of the shelf, fell, and smashed to bits. Once while eating lunch she was observed to move bread across the table and cause it to jump into her mouth.

The tasks which she performed in laboratory experiments and for motion pictures were not always easily accomplished, possibly due to the negative attitudes of people around her. With deep concentration after several hours to warm up her supernormal powers, the tasks assigned by the researcher were performed. The psycho-kinetic feats were made much more difficult by the skeptical attitudes of viewers.

These grueling tests had a very definite physical effect upon her. Her heart beat increased by four times; the beat became arrhythmic; tests showed high blood sugar; and her whole endocrine system was affected. The tests left her drawn and tired. Some tests caused her to lose as much as 4 pounds in a half-hour.

During these well-documented laboratory tests, she has accomplished the perternatural feats of moving matches, salt cellars, apples, and small dishes across a table. Once when asked to move the sand in an hour-glass, she moved the entire hour-glass. A truly dramatic experiment was conducted with a raw egg floating in a saline solution. From across the room, Neyla Mikhailova separated the white from the yolk and brought them back together again. She had previously been accused, by some skeptics, of using magnets or threads to move objects. Since eggs are not magnetic and it would be impossible to fasten a thread to the yolk of an egg, she could not have accomplished this task by such trickery. She demonstrated her psycho-kinetic ability in another way that would also be hard to fake. This consisted of filling a glass jar with smoke, then dividing the smoke in the jar from a distance.

Some Russian scientists believe that psycho-kinesis will be understood by studying the fields of electro-static and magnetic forces which surround our bodies. The scientists checking the magnetic fields surrounding Mrs. Mikhailova have found them to be much greater than those around most people. They reported that when performing her unbelievable feats of psycho-kinesis, these magnetic fields began to pulse as though a wave of energy from her brain caused vibrations. This concentration of energy seemed to be directed by her gaze to the object which she was trying to move, and even though it was non-magnetic, they suspected that in some way magnetic forces pulled it to her or pushed it away.

The Russian scientists have learned much from the tests and experiments conducted with Neyla Mikhailova. And it does not seem likely that they will be satisfied until they have found some way of utilizing this amazing power for the benefit of all mankind.

Without knowing how psycho-kinesis is accomplished, we can follow the concentration technique to move objects for our benefit.

2. TECHNIQUES TO TAP TORNADIC TORRENTS

Power from the sun in the form of thermonuclear energy, has been available on earth for billions of years. During the several billion years of the earth's life, when it was a molten mass of bubbling materials, this energy served no useful function because it could not be used until there was plant and animal life to convert the sunlight into oil, coal, and other forms of fuel.

With the beginning of life, the sun's energy was converted into products needed to support the higher forms of life on earth. But it has been only in recent years that man has understood enough about thermonuclear energy to control it directly for possible space vehicle propulsion or production of electricity on earth.

Like thermonuclear energy, which has been available for billions of years but has only been recognized and utilized recently, psycho-kinetic forces have been available for billions of years, but are now only just beginning to be utilized by some people. When psycho-kinesis is accepted as a force, we shall learn to use it, and when we know how to use the force, we shall. The many people who have tapped this psychic source of energy, have developed techniques which may also help us tap the universal source of energy, if use of this force is within our area of universal responsibility.

By this it is assumed that each individual has physical, mental, and psychic abilities, which qualify him for a particular job in the universe. If he understands his assignment, accepts it, and does it well, he will have great wealth, fame, and happiness, because he will function smoothly in the physical and psychical materials of his universe.

A Place in the Universe

In the same manner that each one of us should determine what our physical and mental talents qualify us to accomplish in this physical existence, we should also determine what our psychic talents qualify us to do in the spiritual existence which is a part of this total universe when we reach the cosmic consciousness level of awareness. Before we begin trying to move objects with our mind, and before we try to know the future, we should carefully examine our motives, talents, and goals in these areas. Just as parents don't give the car keys to the child until he has the ability to drive the car, we may not be given the keys to universal powers until we learn how to use these powers. Like the child asking for the car keys, we should ask for the keys to psychic powers and depend upon the universal father to give us the keys only when we are ready for them.

Some of those people who have apparently accidentally tapped psychic powers, not understanding what they were doing, have suffered damage.

The many accounts of poltergeists throwing objects about at random and destroying some objects may be illustrations of uncontrolled demonstrations of psychic powers. These accounts are often associated with a young person who may cause objects to move. Many religious people believe that these strangely moving objects are controlled by demons, evil spirits, etc. In some cases, the people who are bothered by the poltergeist will ask a priest or preacher to exorcise away the spirit, not realizing that proper use of the psychic power could be of great benefit.

William Niederkorn, writer for the *L.A. Times/Washington Post Bureau,* obtained several interesting cases of uncontrolled psycho-kinesis from Rev. John J. Nicola, who specialized in exorcising out spirits.

One July afternoon in 1971, while sitting in his office completing some of the paperwork required of the assistant director of the National Shrine of the Immaculate Conception in Washington, the Rev. John J. Nicola was interrupted by a telephone call. The voice emanating from the receiver was calmly deliberate—the pastor of a parish in the Virginia suburbs. He wished to consult Father Nicola "concerning a possible infestation or obsession of a couple's home by the devil."

That evening Father Nicola visited the home in question accompanied by the pastor from the suburban church. It was the home of an upper-class family consisting of parents and three children. While the wife served refreshments, the husband began narrating a series of bizarre and seemingly unnatural events that had occurred in their house since they moved into it four months previously.

When the strange occult occurrences first began, the couple attributed the noises they heard—the sound of footsteps running up and down the stairs and moving about the house, knocks on doors, voices calling out of nowhere identical to those of members of the family—to their imaginations. But after a few weeks, more severe and even more inexplicable events occurred.

One night when the family arrived home late after visiting relatives, they had the frightening experience of seeing every light in the house mysteriously flash on and off as they pulled into the driveway.

Another night, just after midnight, the couple were watching television when they heard glass shatter in the kitchen. Upon inspecting, they discovered the pentagonal kitchen clock, smashed to bits, lying face down on the floor. They saw that the 4-inch spike which had supported the clock lay beside it cleanly nipped in two. They said that the nail hole in the wall was clean and the paint and plaster in that vicinity showed no signs of disturbance.

One afternoon while the downstairs maid was waxing the piano stool, the piano suddenly leaped away from her and cut a sizeable dent into the oak mantle of the fireplace.

To explain these events Father Nicola turns to the unusual field of parapsychology, which attributes the unexplained moving of objects to the mind mysteriously controlling psychic forces. Since there were three children in the family, Father Nicola suspected one of them of unknowingly causing the poltergeist phenomenon.

Father Nicola noted that the year 1971 had shown an increase in the number of poltergeist cases. While he had experienced none at all since 1968 for which his assistance had been required, he was called upon three times in 1971. Father Nicola referred to that increase as "dramatic."

In part this increase may be viewed as a reflection of the sensational popularity occult subjects were receiving during that time period, which may have influenced children to experiment with psychic forces.

Father Nicola said, "The problem of our age in tapping higher power is a lack of faith, but personally anything emotional like that scares me off. Blind faith is just another prejudice.

"History shows that at times when there is much Satanism (uncontrolled psychic forces), there is also much good. Other major outbreaks occurred during the time of Christ (devils are mentioned no less than 3,000 times in the *New Testament*) and during the Middle Ages, the time when our great cathedrals were built. I regard our present situation as a doubtfully good thing."

Since spirit forces seem to also do great good even when some damage occurs, it is very possible that misuse of the cosmic force causes the damage; therefore, we should learn how our talents qualify us for use of psycho-kinesis before we use it extensively.

Overcome Reluctance to Try

Considering psycho-kinesis too awesome and dangerous, or nothing but wild ideas will be a stumbling block to developing techniques for controlling it. Based upon the experiences of many people who have developed psycho-kinetic ability, the only requirement for success is effort.

The famous spiritualist medium, Arthur Ford,[1] states he has

---

[1] Ford, Arthur, *Nothing So Strange,* Paperback Library, New York, N.Y., 1958.

observed that all individuals or groups who make a concentrated effort to use universal powers to accomplish some particular worthy purpose would always develop some form of psychic manifestations. He has observed and experienced the psychic forces which are available for curing alcoholics, drug addicts, sickness, etc. He also used these forces many times during his famous career as a psychic to help others, and he gained many intangible rewards.

Yet, it is difficult to stare at an object and concentrate on it moving. It gives you a ridiculous feeling. We know that the object won't move unless we move it with our hand. Our mind has no control over objects, except those attached to it by body fibers, nerves, muscles, etc. So, don't be silly. In spite of such feelings, time after time people who have tried direct mental control over matter have had successful results. Even the writer, who is a trained scientist, knowing that an object can move only if a force is applied, certainly has a difficult time overcoming the reluctance to try direct control, but I have tried with very interesting results.

One night I was staring at a pencil trying to make it rock back and forth. I had just laid the pencil on the table in front of me and observed it rocking as it settled down on a flat surface. Thinking that it would take only a small psycho-kinetic force to rock the pencil, I rested my elbows on the table and concentrated on the pencil rocking. With increased concentration, my anticipation of it moving created excitement which resulted in an unintentional, involuntary twitch of my shoulder muscles. This shook the table which rocked the pencil. And I had the same message which had been given to me before, that my place in the universal system was to use my brain to receive the psychic messages (psycho-kinetic force), and my brain would control my body muscles to move a pencil or other object.

It was difficult for me to overcome my reluctance to try to move the pencil directly with my mind, but when I did, I obtained very satisfying benefits.

A Hex Results in Psycho-Kinetic Powers

While some of us must exert continuous effort to develop our latent ability to control the matter around us with our minds, a few have obtained special benefits almost without intention. This seemed to be the case with a widow from the western part of the United States, a beautiful personality, who was apparently hexed by a person skilled in voodoo.

While managing a girl's boarding house in a western state in 1970, she had to fire a south sea island cook. Shortly after she fired this cook, she began hearing the voice of her ex-employee in her mind threatening her with bodily harm. This unpleasant situation continued through several unusual incidents until the widow became very mentally disturbed and asked God to help her break the hex. Almost immediately following her request for help, she experienced voices in her mind telling her that they would protect her, but even more important, would give her much information, through automatic writing, for her benefit and the benefit of all mankind.

The first convincing display of the psychic power available to the widow came on the first day after the protective voices spoke to her, while the hex voice was still threatening her with physical damage.

The hex spirit voice was telling her on this fateful day that it would cause her to have an accident while driving the car. But the good spirits, now within her mind, were assuring her that they would protect her from the hex spirit.

She felt a battle within her mind, which was won by the sweet protective spirits, who were in control of her complete body when necessary. As she was driving her car down a hill on this triumphant morning, she felt so confident that the spirits had power to protect her that she removed her foot from the brake pedal while going downhill, and the psychic forces brought the car to a stop without even using her body muscles!

Whether the psycho-kinetic force was applied to the brake pedal or the front of the car, she could not tell, but the effect was dramatic. The car was stopped by this mysterious force while the car was going downhill!

But the psychic voices had a word of reprimand for her. They cautioned her not to do that again.

On another occasion, while her daughter was driving their car on a Missouri interstate highway, the car went out of control on the rain-slick road and began to spin around.

The daughter, frightened beyond reason, asked God to help them.

The car skidded to the edge of the freeway, went over, across a ravine, and on to another ramp of an adjacent freeway. It landed upright on its wheels!

As the car left the freeway, out of control, the widow's psychic voices had assured her that they would protect her and her daughter. They did by lifting the car into the air, carrying it across the ravine, and setting it gently down on the other ramp!

She said she felt them and the car floating through the air and coming to rest on solid concrete without even a thud! Mother and daughter had been protected by a fantastic display of psycho-kinetic forces, who responded to the daughter's desperate request to God for help.

From being hexed and threatened by a spirit voice, the widow received the protection and comfort of psychic powers.

She experienced many other manifestations of the fantastic psycho-kinetic powers which she had at her command.

While sitting in bed reading, her ring, which was tight on her finger, gently moved down to the fingertip and returned to its original position.

At the hospital bedside of her brother, dying of cancer, when she was asked to heal him of hiccups, her purse gently moved off her arm and floated down to the floor. Those in the room broke into sobs as they realized that strange psychic forces were available to her. She was able to stop her brother's hiccups, but did not cure him of cancer, because she had already been told that he would die.

As she related to me these fantastic accounts of psycho-kinesis and other mysterious psychic occurrences, I was thoroughly impressed by her beautiful, sweet, calm strength, which convinced me that she had tapped the cosmic powers of the universe.

She felt that God dwelt within her, giving her peace and bliss.

While she gained psychic powers because of a desperate need to combat a hexing spirit, others have gained initial control of psycho-kinesis by playing with a Ouija Board.

Simple Moving of Objects

There is much debate about whether the Ouija Board is helpful or harmful in developing psychic powers. Some people feel they can contact the wrong source of power which will be detrimental, while others feel that the Ouija Board is a stepping-stone to other and better methods of obtaining psychic powers. However, when the Ouija Board is taken seriously, it generally brings positive results. And like other methods of contacting the spirit world, it is more difficult to overcome our reluctance to try, than to obtain successful results.

Many famous psychics first discovered that they could control psycho-kinetic forces while their fingers were resting lightly on the Ouija disc. Usually they were touching the disc along with a partner on the opposite side of the board. As they asked the Ouija questions, the disc would mysteriously begin to move without the conscious effort of the ones touching it. They would be amazed to find that the Ouija would slowly spell out a message as it moved from one letter to another.

Whether the disc moved by psycho-kinetic forces being applied directly to the disc or whether the forces were signals to the subconscious brains of the manipulators is also widely debated, but, apparently, the brains and body muscles of the manipulators were used to amplify the weak signals coming from the psychic realm. If the disc were being pushed directly by a psychic force, it should move without the fingers of the questioners on it.

When a question is asked of the spirit world, the response may come directly to the brain in some type of coded signal. This signal releases photons in the brain, producing brain electrical pulses, which move the muscles of the arms to slide the disc on the Ouija board to the desired letter and spell out the occult message. Such a response seems to be the most reasonable explanation, because a very weak psychic signal could be amplified by the body to move an object.

The Ouija board technique is also closely related to water witching, the swinging pendulum, swaying of the body, automatic writing, mediumship, etc. All of these methods of using psycho-kinesis to move objects requires use of the body to amplify the very weak psychic signal.

A next step, or more direct method of controlling psycho-kinesis, seems to be the table raising or rocking techniques. The table, with the hands of several people resting lightly on it, will begin to move from side to side as if pushed by some invisible genie (or the table could be moved by the people's hands resting on it). But when the table rises directly off the floor, it seems that only direct psycho-kinetic force could accomplish this unless the fingers of the group have somehow become very sticky. Since many people have observed objects moving without anyone touching them, the table movement could also be a result of direct psycho-kinesis; i.e., not being amplified through the brains and muscles of those seated around the table.

We may want to try each of the simple methods of tapping the awesome psychic powers or we may wish to take other more direct measures of utilizing the tremendously beneficial, psycho-kinetic universal forces. Regardless of which method is used, we should spend time trying to develop our own particular method of linking ourselves to the spiritual universe where psycho-kinesis and the wisdom to control psycho-kinesis is available.

A Direct Approach

The primary direct approach to the unobstructed universe is the simple, old-fashioned religious one of first recognizing, or being aware of, a higher intelligent being or beings who may be called God, angels, spirits, masters, controls, etc. At this level of awareness, we must overcome the reluctance to talk to the universal energy intelligence, and when we do, the results will be very satisfying and rewarding to us. But after the initial contacts with the psychic power-house, we must progress beyond the usual religious concepts to that of expecting to have a real mental and physical encounter with the energy intelligence. Where in traditional religion we hear about the power of God, in the true awareness of God, we are a part with universal intelligence, meaning that we have great wisdom, power to move objects with our mind, heal the sick, and perform feats which will bring great benefits to our mental well-being. We can obtain all of these benefits by a sincere desire and continuous effort to know and understand the universal way of life.

Although I recommend the direct approach to universal energy since this has been my method, I have found it an extremely slow way of progressing from initial awareness of a higher power to actually moving objects with my mind.

The direct approach was slow for me because no one told me about the greater power. No one told me that I could ask universal energy intelligence a question and receive a direct answer. I had to find this out by trial and error. I had to discover over a period of 30 years that he was telling me what the future held for me. It took me 30 years to realize the force moving me from a log house on a tenant farm to an estate in the suburbs was the kind, wise, psycho-kinetic power from the psychic universe.

While some people receive the psycho-kinetic power to move objects directly with their mind, I have received psycho-kinetic power to motivate or direct me to the right place at the right time. I had the determination to work hard in school, preparing myself for a vocation designing space vehicles. I had the drive from universal intelligence to write books, spend much time with the family and other people, and do many other useful tasks because the psycho-kinetic force was impressing upon my mind the signals from a much-advanced level of wisdom and intelligence. It was the universal force causing me to make the right decision that obtained the much-sought-after esoteric benefits of wealth, happiness, satisfaction, and recognition, but the primary benefit to me is the feeling of being helpful to others.

The Pendulum Method

Friends of the writer tried the pendulum technique to obtain information with successful results. They were well grounded in the Protestant religion when they began using a pendulum, but they felt that the psycho-kinetic forces were available to move the pendulum; so, they decided to try it as an experiment. They would hold the thread of the pendulum, a needle, in one hand, allowing it to swing back and forth over their other hand or another person's hand. By observing the motion of the needle, when a question with a known answer was asked, they determined which type of motion would be yes and which would be no. Then they asked the pendulum questions about family life and business matters.

The pendulum gave them the correct answers to many business questions for several months. It would give them knowledge about business matters which helped them prosper. From this technique of using psycho-kinesis, they progressed to other more direct methods which have benefited them by expanding their business and increasing their income. They readily admit, as do many who try these psycho-kinetic techniques, that the greatest impedance to success is lack of confident concentration.

As different techniques are tried, one person may be more successful than another. We should persistently pursue those techniques which give the best results, but most of all, press on. We should not hesitate to ask for big items. If we want to be President of the United States, ask for help in becoming President. If we want to take a trip around the world, ask for it. If we want a beautiful house, ask for it. We may not obtain everything we want when we schedule it, but we shall either receive the item or receive a message which will explain why we cannot have it.

One of the areas which requires much help from higher intelligence is in solving personal and family problems. The question of what decisions to make from childhood through adulthood requires more power than the average person has at his command. These questions can be addressed to the universal intelligence, who will help by using psycho-kinetic forces to move people and objects to solve our perplexing personal problems.

It is a fascinating and thrilling experience to ask universal intelligence a question and have very definite answers given to the problem in three or more different ways. This type of experience is presented in the material explaining how light is the window to the spirit universe.

Many techniques can be used to obtain the key to psycho-kinetic power and all its wonderful benefits. These techniques can be used successfully after we determine how we fit into the universal pattern. What are our talents and abilities? But most of all, before any technique will work, we must overcome our reluctance to try tapping the cosmic powers. Fortunately for some people, no particular technique is required because they have special psychic abilities or a spirit being initiates contact with them. Moving small, simple items first, to establish confidence, is a start, but a direct approach to the universal energy intelligence is also very effective. Usually, simple techniques for tapping psycho-kinetic forces progress to better, more effective techniques as we learn that the good, psychic universal forces are readily available with assistance, far beyond our wildest dreams.

Involved in all techniques of approaching the psycho-kinetic powers is contact with other people. It has been shown by many tests that a group working together for a common goal requiring psychic forces can be more effective than one person.

The interrelation between persons, expressed in love and a desire to help another person, is a strong influence in developing techniques to utilize psycho-kinetic power.

Developing the Mystic Element

One of those who has developed psychic powers is David Hoy,[2] a 41-year-old Baptist minister who preached a psychic gospel to packed lecture halls and large radio audiences.

Although David Hoy once said that he did not believe in anything occult, 18 years later he had written four books on the subject and was firmly convinced that ESP was available to everyone who would use psychic powers to make this a better world. He believed that we can develop prophesying powers that will benefit us in every area of living, from helping a housewife find a pair of lost scissors to investing in business ventures and preventing accidents.

Hoy credited pianist Van Cliburn with first introducing him to the occult while Hoy was directing a Baptist youth group in New York and Cliburn was a student at Julliard School of Music and a member of the same church.

A graduate of the University of South Carolina, Hoy earned his divinity degree from Southern Baptist Theological Seminary in Louisville. Then he and his wife Shirley spent a year in Brazil as missionaries.

Although as a young boy he had experienced some "twinges" of ESP, including a premonition of his father's death, he didn't try to develop his abilities. He said he didn't try to improve his ESP, "possibly because my stern religious upbringing as a child made me think I couldn't."

Hoy stopped practicing in the ministry when the board of the Southern Baptist Church turned down his request for a second assignment to Brazil in 1963. He felt that he was turned down because he was considered too much of a radical. Then, after

---

[2] *Huntsville Times,* April 4, 1972.

turning down a rural church assignment, Hoy went to work as a news director for an Evansville, Indiana radio station. Still not satisfied and feeling that ESP was a coming thing, he set out for New York in 1967.

A chance encounter with a friend who was employed by a publishing company led to a contract to write a book on extrasensory party games. Not only has Hoy written two other books and made a background record of how to develop ESP, but he built up a lecture tour of 60 to 70 colleges a year. He also had hour-long weekly phone-in programs with radio stations in Cincinnati, Kansas City, and Pittsburgh.

Hoy, who had accumulated more than $1 million by 1972, repeats that having ESP is "like remembering something that hasn't happened yet. It isn't a picture, it isn't words–it's just there in your mind.

"I tried religion, attempting to pray out to someone in the other world. I tried relying constantly on friends. Neither of these gave me answers to life. ESP has."

Hoy believes that the "mystical element to life" can be developed in everyone. He thinks that it is necessary to have a willingness to depend on the psychic and an ability to look inward.

One builds up confidence in psychic intuitions by keeping track of the percentages of hits and misses, according to Hoy, who rated himself at an 80% accuracy level.

Hoy believed that he had improved his ability to the point where he could pinpoint occurrences and possibly prevent them by using his psycho-kinetic powers. However, up to 1971, he had not been able to prophesy exactly what would happen.

His children played sensitivity games to increase their ESP ability. They did exceptionally well in school, and he believed that much of the credit was due to their ESP abilities.

David Hoy and his family felt that psychic powers had helped in every phase of their life and could benefit others in the same way.

Table Rocking Method

Table rocking is a form of intellectually controlled molecular motion which has given many people information leading to wealth, fame, and happiness. The table moves, at the request of the questioner, to answer a question about the future which results in special gains to the one knowing the future.

Jim Henry who was in public information with the National Aeronautics and Space Administration for several years has conducted many table rocking sessions, since he was ten years old, to obtain information which has led him to be Director of the Chamber of Commerce in New Orleans. He has found that any group can control a table to obtain a higher source of knowledge if they are "believers." A skeptic in the group can prevent movement of the table. He and the group, usually about four, will seat themselves around the table, after turning the lights down and trying to prevent distractions.

He first asks the table to acknowledge that a spirit is present.

The table responds with a movement.

He asks the table to rock once for yes and twice for no. Then he begins asking questions of interest to the group.

During one of these eventful psycho-kinesis sessions, the group consisted of four adults and an active, cheerful three-year-old-child. They were all seated around the table, with the little girl ready to play a game, from her viewpoint. As the table responded to Jim Henry's question, he noticed that the hair on the little girl's arm was standing straight out as if statically charged.

Did the cosmic force which moved the table cause a static field or was the force acting directly upon each hair of the little girl's arm, causing them to stand up? If the force could be increased, would it lift a person?

Jim Henry has harnessed strange occult forces to move a table in response to his question. He has found the information obtained beneficial in his highly successful career.

A Heavier-than-Water Object Floats

A good demonstration of the probable way that the movement of matter by the mind works is the miracle that Elisha performed in causing an axe to float. "On reaching the Jordan they cut down some timber. But as one man was swinging his axe, the head of the axe fell into the water. 'Alas, my master!' cried the man, 'it was borrowed.' 'Where did it fall?' said the man of God. The man showed him the spot. Then, cutting a stick, Elisha threw it in, and so made the iron swim." *(II Kings 6:4-6)*

To cause the metal axe head to float could be done by controlling the movement of water molecules around the axe. Moving the water so that a current carried the axe to the surface would explain how the iron could swim, but moving the molecules of water with the mind is far from being understood.

Other miracles that involve the controlled movement of water are the many cases where water was parted and people walked through on dry land. Also, Jesus walked on water, which would require a much more violent movement of water than floating an axe (see *Matt. 14: 22-23; Mark 6: 45-52; John 6:16-21).*

To have an idea of how much movement of the water would be required to float a man on top, consider a water skier who skis barefoot on the water. This can only be accomplished when the boat is pulling the man at 40-60 mph and there is a fantastic spray of water thrown up around the skier.

Now, instead of the skier moving through the water, assume that by the use of P-K the water can be made to move–strike the bottom of the skier's feet so that he is supported on the water. It would seem that a very violent movement of the water would be required to support the water walker. Rather than a violent moving of the water against the water walker's feet, possibly the molecules of water are held in place by the P-K signal releasing photons in the correct direction and the water beneath the walker's feet becomes as firm as ice.

Of course, the laws of P-K are speculation, but more important is how can P-K power be obtained? The answer should be available from those who have had or who now have P-K ability and the extra-terrestrial beings who probably understand how P-K functions. Not only are there many unusual happenings which seem to be cases of P-K, but often associated with these are reported unusual beings who are called god, angels, messengers, alien beings, extra-terrestrials, ghosts, etc. If we examine the many unusual stories of strange happenings, we shall obtain a more complete idea of how P-K functions, provided we are first convinced that P-K does exist.

The Crowning Act of Mind Controlling Matter

Back in the antiquities of mankind when records of events may have been confused with the imagination of an enthusiastic writer, the story is told of a feat which excels all feats ever recorded of man's power over matter.

During a battle between two armies of mortal men, one side of the conflict was being aided by an extra-terrestrial being called "AM" by the ancient writer. It would seem that thousands of years before mankind had advanced to explosive weapons of war, for a super-intelligence to aid one group of men in battle would bring the fight to a swift conclusion, because, obviously, they would possess superior firepower. Now in this story, even though the battle was being won by Jos, with the aid of AM, who used almost seemingly unsporting tactics, more help was needed. So AM hurled a great missile at the enemy as they fled down a mountain pass.

Using a large chunk of ice as a missile, AM killed more of Jos' enemies, as would be expected, than was killed by Jos' army.

Now in the unenlightened darkness of illiterate mankind, when the success of a great man was measured by the number of men he and/or his army could slay in battle, for the super-intelligence to kill even one more than Jos and his army was indeed a superb show of his lordship.

However, not to be shown up as an inferior killer by AM, Jos, possibly with some assistance from AM, upstaged the hero of all heroes.

Needing more time to obtain a superior quota of dead enemy; throwing all logic to the winds; stretching egotism to the peak of egotism; surpassing the braggarts of all braggarts; uttering with ridiculous authority the ultimate of all commands, Jos COMMANDED THE SUN TO STAND STILL, and the moon, too!

Never before or since has there been written as a true story such a colossal tale of the absurd, immature, rash act of a mortal man, who, for the selfish desire to conquer an enemy or surpass the score of a superior competitor, demanded more time to complete his grim task.

Jos could have asked for a chance to fight another day or for the enemy to flee, or for the enemy to surrender. It would seem intensely logical that an enemy who had hundreds of men killed by giant hunks of ice hurtling down from the sky would be entirely willing, possibly even eager to surrender to Jos, but this is not the way it happened, according to the story. Instead, upon the presumptuous command of a mortal man that the sun and moon stand still, they did!

As impossible as it would seem to enlightened twentieth century laymen and scientists, according to the ancient writer, the sun and moon did stand still, during which time Jos and his army performed their dastardly deed of taking vengeance upon his hapless enemy.

According to the story-teller, the sun stood still and the moon halted until a nation (Jos) had taken vengeance on its enemies, as indeed is written in the ancient *Book of the Upright.* The sun stayed in mid-heaven and made no haste to set for almost a whole day. Never before that time nor since has there been such a day as this day, on which AM listened to the request of a mortal man; AM fought for his chosen people.

Even though some few modern people would consider the possibility that a human mind can control matter, to accept such a story of staying the sun and moon with the mind is certainly beyond man's reason. With our superior knowledge of what it means to stop the sun and moon, we can understand that it is certainly a challenging feat, which must be way beyond the capability of the entire human race, and even with the help of an extra-terrestrial being, certainly that being would require powers far beyond any we can imagine. So, maybe the story isn't entirely factual, even though thousands of people consider it true and many other ancient story-tellers report the same extremely unprecedented phenomenon.

The most unusual writer, Velikovsky, in *Worlds in Collision* writes that many places around the world reported that the sun stood still or there was an unusually long day or night in ancient times.

Has the Sun's Stopping Been Proven?

And in recent years, a noted business manager of an aircraft engine company reported that the missing day of Joshua from the

Bible *(Joshua 10:12-14)* had been found by NASA scientists using computers. This well-educated, worldy, successful, Christian businessman believed sincerely that scientists, while tracing the movement of the sun and moon back into ancient times, had discovered that 23 hours and 20 minutes were missing, unaccounted for in the computed motion of the sun. He understood that at Goddard Space Flight Center, NASA scientists had programmed computers to predict the future position of the sun and moon and the program could also be run back in time to determine where the sun and moon have been any number of years in the past. According to Mr. Hill's story, during a computer run in which the paths of the sun and moon were being traced, when the position had been determined way back beyond the birth of Christ, the computer suddenly stopped.

It would not compute, indicating an error in some data fed into it.

In trying to determine what could be wrong with the program, Mr. Hill said that one scientist recalled the Biblical story of the missing day and inserted this information into the computer. When exactly 23 hours and 20 minutes had been cut from the time in ancient days, the computer again cranked out the paths of the sun and moon until it hit another snag at the time when King Nebuchadnezzar had asked God to move the shadow on the sundial back 15 degrees as a sign that he could live another 15 years.

According to Mr. Hill, by some shrewd calculations, this Biblically well-grounded NASA scientist determined that 15 degrees was exactly 40 minutes, which accounted for the remainder of the missing day. (It would seem more reasonable that 15 degrees on a sundial would be about 60 minutes, since the sun passes through 360 degrees in 24 hours.)

And, so, Mr. Hill proclaimed to the world once again that science had verified a Biblical story. However, some other scientists were very skeptical of Mr. Hill's story, even though they may not have been skeptical of the Biblical story.

This author, a scientist who also works for NASA, saw Hill's story in the *Huntsville News* and was very puzzled about how a computer could do what Hill had claimed. He asked Hill for more specific information as to who the NASA scientists were who had programmed the computer, but Hill was unable to supply any additional helpful information. Hill was unable to remember where he had heard the story. The author verified, with computer experts, that a computer could not find a missing day unless historical records were absolutely accurate, which is not the case.

The computer experts told him that computers are no smarter than the programmers who tell them what to do. The main advantage to computers, the experts explained, is that they are faster and more accurate than the programmers in arriving at the solution to a problem.

This author also investigated sun and moon trajectory work being done by Goddard Space Flight Center and the Jet Propulsion Laboratory. He found no such work being done at Goddard, but Jet Propulsion was doing such work for NASA, although not to the extent that Mr. Hill had reported.

Mr. Hill's story has been repeated many times in newspapers, magazines, church bulletins, on television, and radio, because people wanted to believe that the sun and moon stood still as recorded by an ancient writer. It is extremely important to some people to believe that the Biblical stories are accurate, even to the extent of believing other stories which are inaccurate but seem to prove the Biblical stories.

This author also suspects that the Biblical story of the sun standing still is a true report expressed by a writer who was very limited in his understanding of what he saw.

Any grade-school science student knows that we can see the sun when it is below the horizon because the earth's atmosphere bends the sun rays coming to us. Since the rays pass through more of the earth's atmosphere when the sun is low on the horizon, the rays are bent more than at any other time. So the sun could appear to stand still or be very slow in setting if its rays were being bent around the curvature of the earth so that it could be seen after it was below the horizon. But this would not account for the long day reported in other parts of the world. Any grade-school science student would also know that stopping the sun really means stopping the earth's rotation.

Did P-K Stop the Earth?

The rotational velocity of the earth's surface is about 1,000 miles per hour. If the sun's apparent movement was halted by stopping the earth's rotation, every object resting on its surface would also have to be stopped or these objects would be hurled across the earth's surface.

If the earth's rotation had been stopped or even severely slowed by a stray planet passing near the earth creating a strong gravitational pull, as suggested by Velikovsky,[3] there would have been severe earthquakes, tidal waves, hurricanes, and other catastrophies in nature, and Jos would have been unable to fight.

If the earth's rotation was changed by a superior being's act of P-K, the powers used to slow or stop the earth could also have been used to slow down the objects on its surface. The earth's rotational change would have required a fantastic quantity of energy, which could have come from the individual atoms in the earth and those objects on its surface. How energy within an atom can move the atom will be discussed in a later chapter.

There are various other ways that a superior being could have caused the sun to seem to slow down, but many of the other possible techniques would have been seen only in a limited area on the earth's surface. History indicates that this phenomenon occurred throughout the world.

One of the most direct methods of performing this feat would be with two large space ships. One would block out the sun and the other would have a light of apparent size and intensity of the sun. The ship blocking out the sun would move so that it cast a shadow where Jos and his army fought, and the other would shine a light from the same position above the army for a day.

After the actual sun set, the ship blocking out the sun could move to the east and block out the sun as it came up until it was again at the location of the ship with the bright light. The ships could then quickly turn off the light and depart, leaving the sun to continue on as usual.

Another way, not involving P-K, would have been bending of the sun rays using some form of reflector such as a large satellite high above the earth. Such a satellite has been planned by the United States to give light for cities or armies at night.

The apparent stopping of the earth and moon's motion, seems to be mainly a case of psycho-kinesis experienced by a superior intelligence who responded to Joshua's request. The evidence pointing in this direction is: large chunks of ice had been

---

[3]Velikovsky, I., *Worlds in Collision,* Macmillan, 1950.

hurled down from the sky; Jos said that the Eternal performed the sun-stopping feat; both the sun and the moon stopped, which indicated that the earth stopped rotating; and there are no records of great catastrophes in nature which would be caused by a planet stopping the earth's spin.

Since the Biblical writer did not know that the earth rotated, if he had made up his story, he probably would not have mentioned that the moon stopped. This seemed to add credence to the ancient story.

If we assume that a superior race of universal beings were present at the time of Jos, we can assume that they had the power of P-K for stopping the earth. If they were here then, they may be close enough now to perform feats of P-K for us; however, they may not be required to assist if there is a natural law which does not require the efforts of superior beings for us to move objects with our minds. With many people reporting the sighting of UFO's today, we may assume that superior beings are close, and even though they may not be needed for us to perform P-K, they may be willing to assist us in obtaining knowledge about P-K.

Moving Stones

Since many cases of objects moving without mental control of the observers have been reported, it is probable that some natural law is involved which does not require the direct act of a super-being. One case of mysterious moving rocks was observed by Sanderson[4] in 1928 in Sumatra.

He was sitting on the porch of a friend's house one evening when a small stone mysteriously came out of the darkness, hit the porch floor, and rolled gently to a stop against the wall. And, as mysteriously as the first one came in from the darkness, others came, causing Sanderson concern about who could be throwing pebbles at them. His host assured him that no one was throwing the stones, and he said no stones had been known to hit anyone—certainly very unusual behavior for lifeless stones which seemed to know where they were going and did not wish to hurt people.

---

[4]Sanderson, Ivan T., "*Things*," Pyramid Pub., Inc., New York, N.Y., 1967.

His host did not have any explanation for the behavior of the stones, but he suggested that his guest mark stones with pen or pencil marks and throw them back into the darkness. Others were marked with paint and lipstick provided by the host and they were also thrown back onto the lawn.

To the amazement of those present, within a minute, the stones were back on the porch, once again arriving without hitting anyone. Even more puzzling was the fact that the stones which hit and slowly rolled across the porch were the same ones which had been marked and thrown into the darkness. Why just those stones returned and not others was a mystery as deep as why they moved at all.

Others who had seen the stones in mid-air, reported that they had a mind of their own, changing direction up to 45° in flight as if they were guided. By whom? The host? Could the stones have followed his subconscious desire for them to come to the porch, or was there a super-intelligence who could control the movement of stones through the air? Why would a super-intelligence spend his time night after night entertaining people with such trivial stone throwing? It would seem more probable that the stones were being mentally controlled by the subconscious mind of the host. Thus an example of P-K following some unknown natural law.

The force to move the stones could be from the controlled motion of stone and air molecules which caused the stones to "float" through the air, or be propelled through the air by the directional release of photons, which in turn controlled the movement of stone and air molecules. The controlling signal for the release of photons would be the undiscovered ESP communication signal.

Moving Men by Mental Means

As easily as small stones flew through the air, men have also levitated. And, again, one of the most famous, well-documented, cases of a man who could levitate was Jesus, who said he was not of this world. The first documented hint that he had such powers was when he was talking to another non-earth being, Satan, who took him to the top of the temple and suggested that he float gently to the ground before a crowd of people to prove that he had great powers (see *Matt. 4: 5,6*).

Satan did not specifically say that Jesus could levitate, but said that Jesus' angels would hold him up. This seems to imply that Jesus did not have direct control of the levitation force, but did have contact with the extra-terrestrial beings who had the necessary control. In either case, the end result would be the same; Jesus could control P-K.

If Jesus did not have direct control of P-K, his indirect control was very effective, as he performed miraculous feats such as: changing water into wine; healing many people of various illnesses and physical defects; twice causing a great catch of fish; raising a widow's son, the daughter of Jairus, and Lazarus from the dead; feeding 5,000 people one time and 4,000 people at another time; obtaining tax money from the mouth of a fish; and causing a fig tree to wilt.

After Jesus was killed, he returned to life, passed through the walls of a room, and as a final proof of his tremendous control over P-K, rose through the air, an act far surpassing the feat of jumping from the spire of the temple. As he was preparing to depart from the earth similar to our astronauts' departure, he spoke words of encouragement to those gathered to see him leave, "You will receive power when the Holy Spirit communicates with you. . . ." When he had said this, he was lifted up while they looked on, and a cloud took him out of sight. As he went up, their eyes were looking at the sky, but two men who were dressed in white appeared beside them and said, "Why are you standing gazing? The Jesus who has been taken into heaven will come back just the way you have seen him depart." (see *Acts 1:8-11*).

One who claimed to be from another world, demonstrating fantastic control of unknown forces, said that we can have such power, but extra-terrestrial men who were present when he departed also promised that he would return in a "cloud vehicle." He said that we do not have to wait for his return to have P-K ability but can receive this when the Holy Spirit comes upon us. He has convinced many people that these Biblical stories are true; however, very few people have gone far in claiming the powers which he said are available to us.

For almost 2,000 years many people have believed that men can control matter with their minds, but few have accomplished what they claimed to believe possible. If we shall try the experiment proposed in this book, fantastic progress in P-K may be realized. If we shall not be afraid to report our unbelievable experiences to this writer, they will be distributed to encourage others and ourselves in even greater feats of psycho-kinesis.

The greatest mass feat of levitation was promised by Jesus, who said that people from all the corners of earth and heaven would be drawn up to meet him in the clouds (vehicles?). Billions of us may one day levitate in mass into vehicles waiting in the sky to take us to some utopian planets in this vast universe!

3. WAS LEVITATION USED IN PYRAMID BUILDING?

Standing in the sands of Middle Egypt are giant pyramids which are one of the seven wonders of the ancient world. How they were built by people who had only the simplest of machines and meager architectural engineering skills, remains a mystery.

The most remarkable pyramids are those of Egypt and Mexico. The pyramids in Egypt were built mainly of a hard, rough-hewn limestone, but large blocks of granite are also used, particularly on the outside. Even 4,000 B.C. or earlier, the Egyptians knew the four directions so accurately that the pyramids are placed with the four faces toward the four directions. The pyramids in Egypt appear to date from about 4,750 B.C. to 3,000 B.C., while those in Mexico may have been built around the time of Christ.

It is believed that most pyramids were begun over a sepulchral chamber excavated in the rock and that the work went on during the lifetime of the King who was having it built. The stones in the pyramids were 2 to 4 feet in diameter but facing stones were much larger. The mechanical skills required to cut the stones from solid rock, move them to the pyramid, raise them to such great heights, and adjust them in their proper places continues to baffle the greatest scientific minds. How this architectural miracle was accomplished is a mystery because no mechanical contrivances which could have been used to lift the stones have been found.

Unknown Forces Raised the Pyramids

Although a fabulous number of slaves could have been engaged in this mammoth operation, machines or unknown forces were still needed to move the stones to their final resting places.

According to Herodotus, the ancient historian, the Great Pyramid was built by Cheops. When, no one knows, but the tendency has been to place the date earlier and earlier, with the earliest date being 50,000 B.C. Herodotus estimated that it took 100,000 men working for ten years to make a causeway 3,000 feet long to use for a roadway in moving the stone from the Turah quarries. Possibly the same number of men had to work another 20 years to build the pyramid. Herodotus further describes the method of building by steps and raising the stones from layer to layer by unknown machines, and probably facing the external portion from the top down. The Great Pyramid was built by Chembes or Chalryes according to the ancient historian Diodorus but it was built by Suphis according to Mametho and Eratosthenes. Suphis corresponds to Shufur, which was deciphered from the hieroglyphics or stones discovered by Colonel Vyse in his important investigations of this pyramid in 1835. This monstrous pyramid, when built, was 768 feet square at the base and 482 feet high to the apex. In some mysterious way, the apex has disappeared and the top is now 12 yards square, large enough to land a helicopter or other flying vehicle. Possibly the pyramid has never had a top but was designed to be flat on top.

The solid masonry in the Great Pyramid is estimated to be 82,111,000 cubic feet. These solid stones, 49 feet above the base, have a passage through them running downward at an angle of 26° 41' for a distance of 320 feet, 10 inches to the original sepulchral chamber, the subterranean apartment. It did not end there but continued on for another 52 feet, 9 inches into the rock, although for what strange purpose remains a matter of conjecture.

The sepulchral chamber is 46 feet long, 27 feet wide, and 11½ feet high. From the entrance passage, another tunnel branches off and leads to a maze of other passages and strange chambers. Another chamber is called the queen's chamber, located on exactly the center line of the pyramid 67 feet above the base. It has a peaked roof and measures 17 feet by 18 feet, 9 inches by 20 feet, 3 inches high. Above the queen's chamber and 36.1 feet off the center line is located the king's chamber, which can be reached through a 150-foot passage which branches off the queen's passage. The king's chamber is 34 feet, 3 inches long by 17 feet, 1 inch wide and 19 feet, 1 inch high. This magnificent chamber is lined with red granite, highly polished "single stones," reaching from the floor to the ceiling, and the ceiling is formed of nine large slabs of polished granite entirely from wall to wall. The only furnishings is a tremendous sarcophagus of red granite, so large that it had to have been introduced into the king's chamber when the pyramid was being built.

The Great Pyramid, a tremendously large structure with detailed passages and chambers, would be very difficult, if not impossible, for us to duplicate in spite of all our architectural engineering skills and equipment. The Great Pyramid was constructed in some mysterious way, using knowledge from the brain of some highly intelligent person or persons. What motivated these ancient people with scant knowledge of life after death to undertake a 30-year program to meet these intricate specifications for immortality?

The second largest pyramid was 707 feet, 9 inches square and 454 feet, 3 inches high. This pyramid also has many passages running to strange dark chambers. Many other pyramids were built by the Egyptians who had a very strong faith about what was necessary for immortality. What gave them this strong opinion?

They Learned Less as Pyramids Were Built

Why would the ancient King, Nebuchadnezzar, build a pyramid 235 feet high and 2,286 feet in circumference and dedicate it to the planets? Why did he build it of different colors of bricks? Did this king know about the planets long before a telescope existed? Had the ancient Egyptian determined that some of the "stars" were close to us while others were much farther away?

With an estimated 100,000 men needed to build the Great Pyramid, tremendous problems of feeding, housing, and managing them would be encountered. Among the 100,000 men were skilled stone masons, construction workers, engineers—all part of that tremendous project. Could the narrow Nile Delta support this many Egyptian government employees?

The tremendous engineering task of cutting stones from a quarry without TNT or other explosives, moving these extremely large stones on wooden rollers, and hoisting the stones into their final resting place, seems much more than men 6,000 years ago could accomplish. How the stones were cut from the quarry is a mystery. How the wooden rollers were obtained in the Nile valley where only palm trees grew is also a mystery. The trees could have been cut far away and floated down the Nile, but this would also have required a tremendous crew of men, because the logs would have worn out quickly from the constant cutting of stones on their tops and bottoms.

How were the extremely difficult maze of passages and chambers calculated for the first pyramids and why were the remainder of the pyramids such close copies without improvement? In fact, the later pyramids seemed to deteriorate in quality, even though some were built about 1,700 years after the first great masterpiece. For some unknown reason, the Egyptians seemed to have learned less about pyramid building as they built them. Did the builder build all chambers and passages as the layers of the pyramids rose, without using the passages except to place the mummies? What lights were used to enter the sepulcher? There seems to be no blackening of walls and roofs from smoke.

None of the explanations for the pyramids, why they were built and how they were built, seem to stand up under critical examination. But there are other speculative possibilities which provide a reasonable explanation for the pyramids.

The Mystery of Egyptian Civilization

When first seen in ancient history, Egypt is already old and grey, at the head of a procession of life that is illimitably vast. It is as if it had no beginning. It stands in awesome ancientness, life its product, with its pyramids; in the dawn of civilization, it's a sphinx among the sands or a palm amid the desert of man's development.

At its earliest known existence, Egypt was mature. It possessed the art of writing by a system of hieroglyphics, and the ideographs have passed into the form of phonetics, which normally requires centuries to be developed, a stage of advancement not obtained by the Chinese language to date.

The monuments of Egyptian civilization testify to a most ancient and original race of men who cannot be traced to any line of rootage in another land. From out of the edge of the desert this amazing apparition came as the head of an immense procession of life, issuing out of a past from which the tracks have been obliterated, like footprints in the shifting desolation of the desert sands.

The mind of universal man is a mirror in which Egypt may be seen because the universal storehouse of knowledge reveals the mysteries of her glory. Within this mirror of the universal mind of man are reflected her pre-monumental and pre-monarchical past, during which she was governed by gods–but, much must be inferred. It is impossible from her mythology to establish a starting point.

Perfect art, language, and mythology did not alight ready-made in the valley of the Nile; and if the ascent is not traceable to the Nile, neither is it elsewhere. There is no vestry of proof that the Egyptian civilization was imported from other lands. Their language shows no traces of a derivation and descent from African languages, nor does early Egyptian art seem to imitate that of neighboring lands.

Mythology and Gods

All mythology and religions of the ancient civilizations tell how gods from the heavens took part in the affairs of men. These myths are attempts of the ancient pagans to explain how the world was created and man came into existence. The myths and religious stories are very similar due to a common origin, or they are similar because of a gradual changing and improving of stories to make them more plausible.

The god Prometheus, one of the Titans, a gigantic race who inhabited the earth before the creation of man, according to *Bulfinch's Mythology,* was assigned the task, along with his brother, Epimetheus, of making man. The gods created man in their image, and with the help of Minerva, goddess of wisdom, they gave to man, from the chariot of the sun, the gift of fire, while the Bible tells that God gave man the special gift of a soul. The fire or soul could refer to the special gift or ability that man has of communicating, using a sixth sense, with higher intelligence.

Mythology, in addition to being interesting reading, may also give us a hint of what was happening on earth before recorded history if we analyze the origins of mythology.

The very early famous poets and writers such as Homer, about 1000 B.C., first told about gods and goddesses living on the earth. Where these writers obtained their ideas is not known, but the philosophers have suggested various theories.

One suggestion is the scripture theory, according to which all mythological legends are derived from the narratives of the Scriptures, although the real facts have been disguised and altered. Therefore Deucalion is another name for Noah, Hercules is Samson, Arion would be Jonah. The Dragon which kept the golden apples was the serpent that beguiled Eve. Nimrod's tower was the attempt of the Giants against Heaven. But that theory cannot, without much extravagance, be pushed far enough to account for many of the mythical stories.

Another is the historical theory of mythology's origin. According to this theory, all persons named in the stories were once real persons to whom has been added, through repeated tellings, attributes of super-human beings. Thus the story of Aeolus, the king and god of the wind, who was supposed to have been the actual ruler of some islands in the Tyrrhenian Sea, where he reigned and taught the nations how to sail better and forecast weather conditions. This historical theory seems reasonable in light of the human characteristic of many a story becoming bigger as it is retold.

Another theory proposes that all myths of the ancients were allegorical and symbolical, containing moral, religious, and philosophical truths or historical fact, which over years of retelling became understood as fact. Thus Saturn, who devours his own children, is the same power whom the Greeks call Cronor (Time) which destroys whatever it has brought into existence. And Io represents the endless wandering of the moon.

The physical theory assumes that the primary ancient elements of air, fire, and water were objects of religious adoration, and the principal deities were personifications of the powers of nature. After personifying these elements, it is an easy transition to the notion of them being supernatural gods presiding over the affairs in nature.

All of the four theories which have been mentioned are probably partially true and it is most probable that mythology sprang from all of these theories combined, instead of from any one in particular. Many myths have arisen from the desire of man to account for those natural phenomena which he cannot understand, and some have arisen from a desire to give a reason for persons and places.

Egypt and Its Gods

Very profound scholars have tried to determine the beginning of Egyptian civilization, and some of these have uncovered some very interesting information.

Even the creation story of the Bible may have originated from Egypt where the Nile river flooded yearly. The universal mythical beginnings with waters, and the genesis of creation with man created from dust (mud), may be offsprings of Egyptian parentage.

In the search for the sources of Egyptian civilization, it has been established that their masterful art, language, and mythology were not brought to the Nile area, since these are not traceable to other places, but apparently originated in the Nile valley. This civilization could be the symbolic tower of Babel in the scriptures from which all nations of the world have originated.

Dr. Morton, an American craniologist of the nineteenth century, said, "I was compelled by a mass of irresistible evidence to say that the Egyptians were an Asiatic people. Seven years of additional investigation, together with greatly increased materials, have convinced me that they are neither Asiatic nor European but aboriginal and indigenous inhabitants of the Nile or some contiguous region, peculiar in their physiognomy, isolated in their institutions, and forming one of the primordial centers of the human family."

In *A Book of the Beginning,* it is maintained that the oldest mythology, religion, symbols, and language had their birthplace in

Africa; that the primitive race of Ham came thence, and the civilization attained in Egypt emanated from there and spread over the world. Possibly the Egyptians sent out colonies over the whole world in ancient times. They may have taught the Babylonians astronomy. This idea is supported by the story of Noah in *Genesis*, if it is assumed that the Ark was Egypt, the starting point of all human races.

The mystery of why Egypt should have made great strides in literally moving mountains and shaping them into monuments of titanic majesty may be obtained from the statement of Rameses III, who built a wall 150 feet in depth, 60 feet below ground, and 90 feet above. "I dragged as hills great monuments of alabaster giving them life in the making." Could the "life" have been some means of mental levitation? In building the wall, they transported blocks of syenite, which weighed 900 tons, by land and water. The cathedral of Notre Dame could be placed in one of the halls of the Temple at Karnar as a small central ornament, so vast was the scale of their operation. How did the Egyptian obtain this knowledge for such mammoth undertakings?

In *A Book of the Beginning,* Egypt is considered to be the land where the Homo sapiens species reached its full stature; yet the Egyptians recognized the black race of Africa as being the first of creation. The Egyptians thought they were born of the great one who is in the heavens, while the black race was born of his eye as superior beings.

The gods of Egypt were numerous; some were also recognized in Ethiopia, where in ancient times they used to carry the images of Zeus and other gods from the Temple at Theber to Libya and celebrated a splendid feast of 12 gods. This was done at an annual Ethiopian festival, at which time statues of Egyptian gods were taken into Ethiopia.

Plato, who spent about 13 years in Egypt trying to determine the beginning of their history, reports that they had divine hymns or songs worthy of the deity which were considered to be about 10,000 years old. Going back further into their mythology, many monarchs reigned, and prior to these was the direct dominion of the gods. From the records of two dynasties of gods and demigods which were collected from the Temple Records and rectified by Lepsins, a nineteenth century historian, and from various Greek chronological writers, he traces Egyptian dynasties back 13,820 years.

Herodotus says, "From the first king to the priest of Vulcan (Ptah) who last reigned, there are 341 generations of men; and during these generations, there were the same number of priests and kings. With 341 generations being equal to 11,340 years, they said that in the past 11,340 years, no god had assumed the form of a man; neither had such a thing happened before or afterwards in the time of the remaining kings of Egypt." This certainly implies that gods in the form of men ruled in Egypt in ancient times.

Herodotus found that the priests claimed to have made chronological observation during a period of about 52,000 years!

It was in Egypt that the transition from mythical gods to one god also took place. Ra, the ram-headed deity, also called Amen-ra of Thebes, together with Nun and Khan, some older gods, were merged into an image of the one god, the Amen of hymns, in which he is celebrated as the one in his works, single among the gods, the one maker of existences, the one alone with many hands, and the one alone without peer.

Ra is credited with saying, "I say a great thing; listen! I will teach you the nature of eternity." And supposedly the Egyptian eternity was Eonian, who had been the timekeeper of its cycles and master of its mysteries, the builder of the ark of the Eternal, who was born to rebuild it and cover it with fresh figures.

Today we may find similarities to a space vehicle for a space traveler in these expressions of what was happening over 12,000 years ago in Egypt.

Apparently, Egyptian civilization is more than 40,000 years old. Possibly up to about 12,000 B.C., beings superior to the Egyptians ruled the people. These superior beings taught many advanced concepts to the Egyptians which gave them the ability to build outstanding monuments, even by today's standards. Only scraps of information are available to give us some ideas of why these great monuments were built. The Egyptians may have been taught how to use P-K to build their pyramids.

Were the Pyramids a Public Works Project?

Although the most widely accepted reason for the building of the pyramids is for funerary monuments for the early pharaohs, Mendelssohn[1] takes exception and proposes that the pyramids

[1]Mendelssohn, Kurt, "A Scientist Looks at the Pyramids," *American Scientist,* Vol. 59, March-April, 1961.

were built as a national economic endeavor. He thinks that some venerated personality with great engineering ability sold a king on the idea of building the pyramids to unify the kingdom and bolster the national economy. He thinks that the first pyramid was Zoser's Step Pyramid at Saggara, and with each additional pyramid built, there were improvements up to the fifth pyramid, which he thinks was the Khufer or Great Pyramid at Giza. After this, the pyramids became smaller and of poorer construction according to Mendelssohn.

After the first project was started, it required about 100,000 men; and to continue government employment on an even level, he thinks the Egyptians continued to build other pyramids at a rapid pace. With the 100,000-men force, Mendelssohn surmises that the six largest pyramids were built in less than a century, after which the pyramids rapidly became smaller and shoddier. After the start of the national effort, pyramid building became an economic necessity whether or not there was a pharaoh ready to be buried. Mendelssohn thinks that the Egyptians invented the state, a form of centralized and efficient organization, which up to then was unknown to the human race.

During the time of pyramid building, Egypt's prosperity increased rapidly, apparently because employment was high.

With 100,000 men producing no useful product which others could purchase, it seems impossible that the prosperity could be a result of the government public works project.

Mendelssohn also proposes that the Mexican pyramids were built for the same economic reasons, although the real secret may be better revealed in the legends of Mexico, which were the same as Egypt. Mendelssohn admits that legend ascribes the building of the large pyramids of Egypt and Mexico to the inspiration of an outstanding sage, who further taught the natives many of their arts and crafts. Legend says that the sage was deified and would return to Mexico from the East. No tombs have been found in the Mexican pyramids, although one may be in the Pyramid of the Sun.

Mendelssohn's theory seems weak, and the mystery of the great pyramids of the world remain—although a theory that extra-terrestrial life influenced pyramid building may be reasonable in light of present-day knowledge of life in the universe.

Science Looks at Life in the Universe

Was a superior extra-terrestrial life responsible for the building of Egyptian pyramids using P-K or some other powerful forces, and were supreme beings responsible for the myths about Gods? Turning to the scientific possibilities of life in the universe, and even the possibility of advanced life already far into its space age when the Egyptian civilization began, we shall examine what scientists have discovered about the universe.

The universe is over 11 billion years old by the latest scientific calculations and measurements, while the earth is only about 4.7 billion years old. This difference of over 6 billion years provides a long time for life to have developed elsewhere in the universe before it developed on earth. Regardless of how life came into existence on earth, it could have come into existence elsewhere in the universe much earlier. The universe has billions of suns similar to our sun which can have planets similar to our earth. It has been estimated by some cosmologists that possibly billions of earth-like planets exist in the universe on which life, as we are, could exist. With so many possibilities of life, it would be an extremely unusual case for life to have developed on this planet first.

Observations which have been made of the universe at great distances from us indicate that laws of nature observed at these distances are the same as they are here. For instance, the law of gravity and the behavior of light, seem to be the same wherever observed in the universe. These scientific observations would lead us to assume that other natural laws which have not been observed at great distances could also be the same throughout the universe; therefore, the natural laws involving the origin of life on earth could apply to over 100,000 other planets in the universe.

When a planet is ready for life, it develops, is seeded, evolves, or something occurs—thus resulting in intelligence as we have it on earth. During the approximately 6 billion years before there was this earth in the universe, many other planets were passing through the phase which produced life on earth.

Probably many planets produced life. If only one planet produced life during the first 5 billion years of the universe, this life would have had over 5 billion more years to expand into space, as we are now doing, before the earth reached the Egyptian period.

Assuming that the earth's civilization continues its technological growth for another 5 billion years, we should be spread throughout the entire universe, if there are natural laws which will permit us to travel at a greater velocity than light. We should someday visit many civilizations in the universe which will be similar to Egypt 40,000 years ago. To assume that advanced universal civilizations have not visited the earth during its life period is statistically highly improbable. Once this conclusion has been reached, many mysteries recorded in history, myths, religious stories, etc. about acts involving P-K begin to make sense.

For those who consider the Biblical stories to be factual, many proofs are given that extra-terrestrial life, usually called angels, was on earth during the rapid development of civilization. Today many people with knowledge of space and space travel have assumed that gods, angels, God, etc., are astronauts who visited the earth.

Genesis' God an Astronaut?

Jean Sendy, a Frenchman, in six books written during the sixties, expounds the theory that the God of *Genesis* was a team of astronauts. He admits that his story is supposition, but feels that it fits the Biblical evidence better than any other idea. He proposes that the *Book of Genesis* contains an ancient and literal tradition preserved intact because of it sacredness to the Jews, who recorded events which began at the end of a period of glacial catastrophe that possibly affected the solar system.

Theology scholars generally agree that the Hebrew word for the "God" who created heaven and earth in *Genesis,* chapter 1, verse 1, is "Elohim," an honorific plural. But Sendy takes it more literally to mean "gods," which is separated from other usages in the same chapter. Other words for God are "Adonai" and "Yahweh," which are singular and describe the individuals in the astronaut team.

Sendy speculates that the "gods" came in a space ship about 18 square miles large, after a journey of about 6,000 years, during which time the originals, approximately 15 couples, were replaced by their descendants, who continued the journey. Since the arriving astronauts had lived their lives in a weightless environment, Sendy thinks they stopped off on Phobos and Deimos, the moons of Mars, to become gradually accustomed to gravity. Before landing on earth, they may have had to clear a path through the clouds completely surrounding the earth, during the windy, waterless, darkness of the last Ice Age, when conditions may have been more like those on Mars or Venus.

During their stay on earth, Sendy thinks these astronauts behaved exactly as all other astronauts do in fact or history. He speculates that they fenced off an habitable area, which may be what is called the Garden of Eden in the Bible. In this paradise, they possibly created a technological society, measuring time as day and night and using cosmic calculations which have mysteriously been part of ancient knowledge ever since. He proposes that they channeled rivers, irrigated land, domesticated animals, and established agriculture.

This is precisely what happened in Egypt during the time when myths tell about gods on the earth.

These long-ago astronauts may have selected specific earthmen as assistants and apprentices, teaching them many new mysteries, among which may have been the secret of levitation which permitted them to accomplish great feats of building pyramids and other tremendous monuments. The astronauts selected one man, Adam, who either learned too much or learned how to do something which was too dangerous for him to handle.

Adam may have been taught by an astronaut (Satan-Lucifer) who wanted Adam to know too much. Then to prevent Adam from doing great damage or learning enough so that he would be immortal, he was expelled from the fenced area, but he already knew how to farm and domesticate animals. With this knowledge, civilization made great strides in the Nile valley.

Sendy thinks the extra-terrestrial beings recreated, "out of the dust" of the caves in which the earth natives had always lived, the new civilization. Since these cave people were completely ignorant of reproductive processes, Sendy thinks they would have expressed a woman as being "created" out of a particular limb of Adam's.

After several millennia, the gods left earth, according to

Sendy's theory, because their research had been completed, their ships needed refueling, or for unknown reasons. It may be that the astronauts knew that man had not advanced sufficiently to continue their contact with him, but possibly in another 10,000 years they could establish contact again. Before leaving they may have completely destroyed their base by inundating it, particularly if it were in the Nile valley, or they may have destroyed it by some other method.

They destroyed all the people whom they had educated, except Noah, because all but Noah were misusing their advanced knowledge to enjoy sins of the flesh. These educated natives may have been tampering with genetics in their offspring to produce giants, geniuses, and other unusual men and freaks. The astronauts saw that much damage was being done and destroyed their students, except for Noah and his family.

But after the flood, Sendy maintains, Noah wanted to continue contact with the space ship and he built an altar, a receiving set. Several years later, the descendants tried to improve upon the receiving set by building a tower-antenna, but the messages they received were confusing to them and they abandoned their venture.

Sendy thinks Noah received a final message from the departing beings, who told him that they would place a "sign of the covenant in the clouds." Using his space age logic, Sendy assumes that the location of such a "sign" would be the moon, and he predicted that NASA would find some message from our ancient visitors. He thought that the message would be in a "negative mass concentration" found by *Orbiter V*—a giant hollow which could have been a site for their original lunar base.

What Sendy called "negative mass concentration" was nothing more than large craters on the moon, and NASA has found no message except those of nature from examining the rocks and terrain.

But that message may still be there for our astronauts, maybe in the form of knowledge about ESP.

Astronaut Ed Mitchell performed an ESP experiment on *Apollo 14* and obtained remarkable results.

Psycho-Kinesis Message in Space

A levitation experiment may yield unusual results in space where a minute force could easily move an object. Since neither NASA nor any government agency recognizes parapsychology as a subject for scientific research, the experiment would have to be conducted by an astronaut as a personal endeavor, like Ed Mitchell's experiment. If the experiment proved a success, as astronaut Mitchell's experiment did, we shall have received another message from above the clouds.

The type of message an advanced race would leave for us should be one which requires more than average intelligence to understand. Maybe the message, "The sign in the clouds," is something which we shall discover in space, not a placard stating that we had "visitors," but a discovery of how to use the powers which they used while visiting us thousands of years ago.

In the quest to determine whether life is unique to earth or a common occurrence throughout the universe, research institutions, including NASA, have been examining many objects obtained from space for evidence of life. NASA has carefully examined the rocks brought back from the moon, searching for any sign of life, but none has been detected. The scientists have discovered a strange phenomenon which has not yet been explained.

When moon dust, which is not soluble in water, is sprinkled around growing plants, they grow much better as if they had been fertilized, even though none of the dust could have nourished the plants since plants can only utilize food in liquid form. Either plants can use the dust in some unknown biological manner or they are responding to the special attention they receive. Plants grow better if loved and given attention, as has been demonstrated many times, particularly by Cleve Backster.[2]

Not knowing what forms of life may be found in space, NASA quarantined the first four *Apollo* crews returning from the moon. NASA considered the possibility of minute life on the moon which could have been carried back with the astronauts.

---

[2]Backster, Cleve, "Evidence of a Primary Perception in Plants," *International Journal of Parapsychology,* Vol. X, winter, 1968, No. 4.

Possibly such life, alien to earth, could have developed rapidly, causing a fantastic catastrophe—but no life was found; therefore, *Apollo 15* and subsequent crews were not quarantined.

Yet dust from the moon caused plants to grow rapidly as if the dust, which was insoluble in water, were a fertilizer.

NASA's Search for Life in Space Is Successful

NASA has been searching for life from space in the meteors which blaze a fiery trail through our atmosphere and bury themselves in the earth. NASA scientists have reported that they have found chemicals of apparent extra-terrestrial origin which are new evidence that life exists elsewhere in the universe. The scientist reporting the discovery to the 162nd national congress of the American Chemical Society in September, 1971 was Dr. Cyril Ponnamperuma.

Dr. Ponnamperuma and a team of NASA scientists had found strange chemicals from the Orgueil meteorite which fell in France in 1864. They were aware that this meteorite was itself the source of a well-known hoax played by practical jokers who inserted organic material into the space rock. They found some of the old planted chemicals, but they also discovered six amino acids and eight types of pyrimidine chemicals. They surmised that both groups of chemicals originated somewhere in the mysterious depths of space. This group of scientists, working at the Ames Research Center of the National Aeronautics and Space Administration in Mountain View, California, had already found, twice before, evidence of life-related chemicals in meteorites, the remnants of shooting stars.

These space visitors were believed to have originated in the belt of asteroids which are in an orbital path outside of the Mars orbit. They are as old as the solar system, about 4.7 billion years.

The NASA scientists reported that the chemicals they discovered were pyrimidine similar to the life pyrimidine molecule which is one of the principal building-block molecules of the DNA genetic code chain, the building block of virtually all living organisms. They said that the chemicals found in the three meteorites were so similar to, but not exactly like the chemicals found in living organisms on earth, that these space-traveling chemicals could easily be considered constituents of an extra-terrestrial life form.

Based upon physical laws which can be observed far into the mysterious depths of space, being everywhere the same; the chemicals which constitute life systems being found in meteorites; stories of gods visiting the earth; UFO sightings; contacts with the spirit world; and other factors—there is strong evidence that advanced life systems should have visited the earth long ago, leaving their secrets of psycho-kinesis along with many other fantastic powers. With powers of P-K and knowledge gained from extra-terrestrial beings, the Egyptian pyramids would not seem to be such an impossible task for that ancient race. With P-K, no machinery would have been required to mine, move, and lift the gigantic stones into place.

Egyptian civilization played a very important part in the rise of Christianity. It was in Egypt that Moses, the Hebrew law giver, gained his education in the courts of the powerful, fearsome Pharaoh.

Moses heard a voice from a burning bush which could have been controlled by the P-K of an extra-terrestrial being. He had power to bring many plagues upon the luckless Egyptians. He was protected and guided by a cloud-like vehicle, which produced a column of light at night, for 40 years in the near vicinity of Egypt. He talked many times with a being who was not of this world. And when Moses was old, he did not die as normal men, but an extra-terrestrial being said he would take care of his body. Moses was seen hundreds of years later beneath a large vehicle (cloud) from which an unearthly, booming voice was heard, proclaiming that the extra-terrestrial being called Jesus was a member of the universal race.

From the Bible stories, we recognize that extra-terrestrial beings who had P-K powers were very active in and around Egypt for thousands of years.

If an extra-terrestrial race wanted to leave a time capsule for us, what would be better than a pyramid?

Why did the Egyptians save the life of an extra-terrestrial being when he was a human biological baby?

Joseph fled into Egypt with Mary and baby Jesus to save Jesus from being slain by King Herod. They were in Egypt for two years or more during Jesus' youth.

What happened while Jesus was in Egypt? Did he have contact while there with other extra-terrestrial beings?

Why was Jesus' body placed in a stone sepulcher which approximated the pyramids built to gain immortality for the Pharaoh?

Jesus was immortal; the stone was rolled away from the sepulcher by an extra-terrestrial being; and Jesus left the earth in a cloud vehicle just like the one that had been near Egypt with Moses for many years.

As Egyptian myths tell how immortality was possible by mummifying a body and wrapping it in cloth, the Bible tells how Jesus' body was anointed with spices, wrapped in cloth, and placed in a sepulcher. Jesus proved to be immortal. Egyptians were told how to be immortal and how gods would return to earth!

When Edgar Cayce, the famous Sleeping Prophet, was asked, while in a trance, "How was this particular Great Pyramid of Giza built?", he replied, "By use of those forces in nature as make for iron to swim. Stone floats in the air in the same manner. This will be discovered in '58." (July 1,1932.) Was it? In 1968 I proposed the theory of intellectually controlled molecular motion which is a possible explanation for moving of objects with the mind, but as of now there has been no accepted discovery of how stones float in air or iron swims. Such a discovery could have been made in 1958 without the scientific community being aware of it.

The extra-terrestrial beings who performed P-K feats taught earthmen how to gain P-K powers. Many humans have mastered the requirements to control matter with their minds, and apparently everyone who follows their instructions can also gain psycho-kinetic powers. These instructions will be given in a later chapter, but it should be understood by the reader that the author does not guarantee success since the purpose of this book is to persuade readers to try the recommended techniques and inform the author of the results. Consider the exercises for improving mind control over matter as experiments to substantiate or disprove a theory of a scientist who has spent many years researching the psychic field.

Ideas of how the ancient, mysterious Egyptian pyramids may have been built using levitation has presented evidence to support the theory that extra-terrestrial beings have used P-K on earth and have taught earthmen how to use psycho-kinesis.

4. SOURCE OF COSMIC POWER

When the tremendously powerful *Apollo/Saturn V* vehicle lifts off its launch pad at Kennedy Space Center in Florida, to those observing, there is no doubt that a fantastic amount of power is generated. Three miles from the vehicle, the noise is deafening, the earth shakes, and a column of brilliant flames, longer than the 340-foot vehicle, blind the observer's eyes. The power to move the monstrous 6-million pound space ship comes from the burning of common and not-so-common chemicals carried in the vehicle. The vehicle's first stage, called the S-IC, uses the common chemical, kerosene, while the next two upper stages, called the S-II and the S-IVB, use the exotic element, liquified hydrogen. All stages burn their chemical with liquid oxygen carried in the tremendous-size vehicle tanks.

The power of 7½ million pounds thrust for the S-IC stage, 1 million pounds thrust for the S-II stage, and 200,000 pounds thrust for the S-IVB stage is produced by a chemical reaction well-understood by rocket propulsion engineers and scientists. The power for the other smaller stages of the *Apollo/Saturn* vehicle used for orbiting, landing, and leaving the moon is produced by other chemical reactions, also understood by the rocket propulsion engineers.

Space Vehicle Power

The power required for the vehicle which picked up Elijah thousands of years ago is unknown, although a fire was associated with that power. When the "cloud vehicle" was with the children of Israel for over 40 years, the power for its generation was associated with a pillar of fire. And when a superior being, God, landed on Mount Sinai to give Moses the laws, the power of that vehicle was associated with much fire, smoke, and noise. Although the power that moved the vehicles used by our space visitors thousands of years ago was associated with fire, light, and noise, much like the *Saturn V* moon vehicle, surely their vehicles were much more powerful, with a tremendously more sophisticated power source.

UFO's, supposedly the vehicles of visitors from space, which have been seen by many people in recent years, have almost always produced light but are usually completely noiseless. One such evasive visitor was seen by the niece of a NASA scientist, a business associate of the writer. This strange incident occurred in 1968 near Birmingham, Alabama.

About dusk one evening of a clear, beautiful, southern day in the fall of the year, two teenage girls had completed a pleasant horseback ride and were stabling their proud steeds for the night. One of the girls, about 14 years of age, had difficulty with her horse as she led it into the stall to remove its saddle and bridle.

The horse behaved in a peculiar way as if it sensed some unseen alien thing.

When the 14-year-old girl came out of the stable, she saw to her amazement a weird, fantastic vehicle moving along just above the treetops.

This uncanny UFO was shaped somewhat like the point of an arrow, yet it resembled the body of an aircraft. As it glided stealthily along, it produced no noise at all, even though it was so low that it seemed to be close enough to hear its engines if it had any.

As this shocked young girl stared at the inconceivable visitor, she saw circular lights along the length of the vehicle, reminding her of windows in our aircraft, but the fateful sight was shaped like nothing she had ever seen before. She shouted for her friend, who was still in the barn, to come quickly and see this enigmatic UFO. Her friend arrived in time to witness the mysterious vehicle silently disappear behind the treetops.

The excited girls told their parents what they had seen, and the NASA scientist's brother, one girl's father, quizzed them at length about their story but found no flaw in it.

Oddly enough their story was later corroborated by a group of children in another section of Birmingham who reported that they saw an arrow-shaped vehicle traveling in the opposite direction to the vehicle observed by the two girls. Both sightings were at approximately the same time.

This strange visitor apparently used power which produced light but little noise. The same type vehicle has been reported by numerous people at other times and places. One such vehicle was seen by the writer's brother near Elizabethtown, Kentucky. This story is given in *Cosmic Mysteries of the Universe.* The weird vehicle he saw had what seemed to be lighted, round windows, made no noise, and was shaped like an aircraft fuselage.

The sizes of these vehicles could not be determined nor even estimated, but one such colossal vehicle was measured during World War II.

A visiting evangelist related to the author an experience which he had during World War II. He was in a bar, prior to his conversion to Christianity, near a service men's training center where he had been entertaining for the United Service Organization (USO). He was with a group of service men, one of whom commented on the unfortunate mental condition of another service man who seemed to have consumed an excessive amount of alcohol.

They said the inebriated fellow had sufficient justification for drinking to excess because he was trying to forget the unexplainable phenomenon he had observed while tracking a routine weather balloon. They reported that he and two other weathermen had been observing and plotting the motion of a weather balloon as it ascended.

When the balloon was several thousand feet high, one of the trackers, the now drunk service man, saw an inconceivable, monstrously large, circular vehicle far above the slowly ascending weather balloon. He brought the attention of the other two men to the UFO, and after recovering from their initial shock, they measured the size and altitude of the unearthly visitor with their tracking equipment.

The vehicle measured 75 miles in diameter, and it was 200 miles from the amazed earthlings. Imagine the power required to move a vehicle of this magnitude through the vast distances of space!

Some far advanced power source is apparently available to propel such a tremendous space vehicle.

But the story of the mammoth vehicle did not end here, because the three excited service men reported the sighting to their superior, who in turn relayed it on to others. The three men were ordered to discuss their strange sighting with no one. The reasons for these instructions were speculated upon by those telling the story to the USO entertainer. They felt that the armed forces leaders were afraid of the public's attention being turned away from the war effort and the armed forces activities, to the visitation from outer space.

The military leaders thought that national attention focused on UFO's would take attention and money away from the war effort. The leaders also had knowledge of many sightings of small UFO's about the time the large one was spotted. They theorized that the large ship was the home base for the small scout ships.

Aside from the many other interesting possibilities the story presents, one prime consideration here is that a colossal amount of power was required to move these space ships, yet, whatever that power was, it apparently did not produce noise and fire like the powerful *Saturn V* moon vehicle, or the 75-mile diameter vehicle would have been observed by a large portion of the earth's population.

One of the reasons why there is so much doubt that UFO sightings are of real vehicles is the lack of noise from these strange vehicles as they travel at fantastic speeds, change directions quickly, and sometimes suddenly disappear with a blinding flash of light as if they had exploded.

Many UFO sightings are lights only, with no visible vehicle or solid material near the lights. These UFO's make no noise, and many observers believe there is no material associated with the light, which again raises interesting questions about how light can exist without a source; i.e., something providing light, like a chemical reaction or gases heated to luminescence. But again the primary question is what power source is available to produce the light.

The Source of Energy on Earth

Automobiles, airplanes, ships, space vehicles, and the majority of other land, air, water, and space vehicles use chemical energy to move them. These vehicles release chemical energy from compounds which are consumed in the power plants of the vehicles.

The chemical energy which is available to power the vehicle was stored in the compound and its elements possibly millions of years ago. As an example, the fuel for the automobile comes from the depths of the earth. The fuel is refined from crude oil which is the residue of decayed plants of millions of years ago. This chemical energy has remained bound up in the underground oil deposits waiting for the human being to learn how to use it and release it. This energy had as an original source the sun, which provided energy for the plants to develop.

Another form of very common energy is electricity produced by water power, burning of coal, natural gas, and nuclear fuels.

Water power is again a by-product of the sun's energy, which evaporates water and lifts it into the sky where it falls back to flow through the water turbine producing electricity.

Nuclear energy is the power released when heavy, radioactive elements decay (split) into lighter molecules. Possibly about 4.7 billion years ago, when this solar system evolved, these heavy elements were formed in the very hot star which threw off large quantities of gases. These hot gases containing radioactive elements formed the planets of the solar system including earth. Therefore, nuclear energy has as a source the sun.

Continued investigation into the sources of all known forms of energy will reveal the only source to be the sun or other stars in the universe. This does not mean that a sun is the only source of power in the universe, just that we do not know of other power sources at this time.

In considering other possible sources of energy, we might

assume that the next logical source would be some other object or system in the universe. But when we look for such a power generator, it cannot be found because all that we can see with giant telescopes beyond this solar system are stars in all stages of development from birth to death.

One very interesting object discovered in 1971 by a space vehicle experiment was an x-ray star only 10 miles in diameter. This object was detected by an experimental device which was placed above the earth's atmosphere by a research rocket vehicle. The strange black object was detected because it released extremely strong x-ray energy which could be detected above the earth's x-ray absorbing atmosphere. Even though this mysterious object was only 10 miles in diameter, it had the mass of our sun, which resulted in a fantastically dense material weighing 40,000 billion pounds per cubic inch. Instead of this object possibly being a source of energy to build suns, it is apparently a dying sun producing x-rays from a plasma of primary nuclear particles, which were elements early in that star's life, but they lost their identity as atoms as the star "burned out." The x-ray star is considered a "cinder" of a once bright, hot energy source for the planets in its solar system.

All forms of energy which have the sun as a source are controlled by a knowledge of how to release this energy. We have learned through research and experimentation that all forms of energy are very useful if controlled, but very harmful if not controlled. When a new form of energy is discovered, it is very possible that we shall have to learn how to control it or it will be harmful to us.

Even the sunlight or photons from the sun are deadly if not properly protected against. A person not used to the direct sun's rays can be sunburned badly enough to die.

The Mysterious Photon

The primary form of energy from the sun is the photon, a small bundle of light which travels at 186,000 miles per second. The photon is produced in an atom when an electron drops to a lower energy state (orbit).

In the sun billions and billions of electrons are dropping in energy levels as the atoms move to the surface of the sun, after these atoms were heated and thus raised in energy level by thermonuclear reaction in the core of the sun.

The thermonuclear reaction is the combining of lighter elements, primarily helium and hydrogen, into heavier elements. Therefore, the source of the photon energy in the sun is hydrogen. The source of hydrogen is unknown, although it is found everywhere in space.

Hydrogen in open space is theorized by cosmologists to collect due to gravitational attraction between atoms and form stars. But the source of hydrogen which seems to remain constant in space is a mystery. It seems as if hydrogen in space is being spontaneously generated from nothing; however, it is more probable that hydrogen comes from some as yet undiscovered source. This source could be the psychic force which moves matter in a strange way. Another source of hydrogen may be light, which is known to form an electron and positron or positive electron in a pair production reaction. With positive and negative charges, basic building blocks of atoms are present.

But somewhere in space, before the stars existed, there had to be a source of photons to produce hydrogen. These photons could have been produced by psychic power, which has been reported by many people throughout history.

The photon, light, is mysterious because there are so many unanswered questions about it. It is peculiar because it behaves as a particle, but also as a wave motion. It does not require a medium for traveling, but zooms like a projectile. It has only one velocity. It never exists at rest. It comes into existence in an atom by some unknown triggering mechanism, and it is absorbed as mysteriously by another atom. The photon is the most common, natural energy source available to twentieth century earthmen, but a better, natural, universal source may be readily available to universal man.

Is One Source of Photons Psychic Power?

The statement "God said let there be light" may be the first message to earthbound man that light, matter, and all physical material has a source in the psychic universe which is undetectable to human beings. This may mean that one source of light is from an unknown universe. And the source of that light has been termed "ether," "orgone energy," "eloptic energy," "tachyons," "neutrinos," etc.

Several years ago, ether was considered to be necessary for light transmission like air or other material is necessary for sound transmission. Ether was defined as an odorless, weightless, resistanceless fluid which permeated all of the universe. Although not considered a source of power, ether was believed to be necessary for the propagation of light by the scientist.

In a very important experiment called the Michelson-Morley experiment, it was proven that no ether existed, or at least that light did not require a medium for propagation. However, the idea has persisted, primarily in the occult realm, that some energy or power source totally permeates the universe, and this unknown is often referred to as ether, although not the ether which was proven not to exist by Michelson and Morley.

In the religious community, there is also the firm belief that power is readily available from an unknown source which can heal the sick, allow a person to walk on water, rise through the air, etc. Of course their belief is that God has all power, but most religionists never consider what or how much power is made available to those who qualify for it. They believe that God decides who can have this power and He only gives it to those who are obeying Him. This religious power is considered to be administered by the Holy Spirit, which is one of the three prime characteristics of God.

The Holy Spirit communicates with man, aids men as considered necessary by Him, and is the power for the many miracles which can happen, according to religionists. The Holy Spirit is not considered to be a subject for scientific investigation by most religious people, nor would He be detectable by scientific means; however, using other names for the Holy Spirit, most courageous people have given specific names to a psychic power and have built equipment which they claim taps the universal power.

One of these machines is called the Hieronymus[1] machine after its inventor. The machine is supposed to pick up and amplify eloptic energy.

---

[1]Hieronymus, T.G., U.S. Pat. Off., Pat. No. 2,482,773. Patented Sept. 27, 1949.

Eloptic energy, according to Hieronymus, is related to electrical energy and optical (light) energy, hence the word "eloptic." This strange energy supposedly carried knowledge and healing power which can be amplified in this machine built by Hieronymus.

The machine, which picks up and strengthens the eloptic energy, is a radio amplifier with a plate for an output instead of a speaker. It was originally built by Hieronymus to identify material which was first calibrated by the machine to a known material, such as gold.

The gold was placed in the detector part of the machine, which was a cylinder attached to a radio frequency local oscillator. (Compared to a radio, the can would be the receiving antenna.) The gold caused a particular reading on a meter which was then marked for gold. Then other known materials were placed in the can and the meter readings were also recorded. Finally, the unknown material was placed in the can and the meter read to determine the nature of the unknown substance.

The machine had one additional very significant feature. Its output was connected to a black plastic plate which was touched by the operator. As the machine was tuned, the operator stroked his fingers lightly over the plate until it felt tacky or sticky to him, then he took the meter reading. The tacky feeling was the primary key in operating this psychic machine, because the feeling was apparently a mental reaction rather than an actual change on the part of the material making up the plate. When the operator thought he felt a tacky plate, he was tuned to the material in the can—and the calibrated meter told him the material's name.

The Hieronymus machine could do much more than identify materials, as would be expected of an occult device. It could diagnose the physical well-being of a person by placing any parts (hair, saliva, etc.) in the can and reading the meter calibration for a normal person. Even a picture of a person placed in the can would give the condition of the person, according to Hieronymus.

But did this machine actually do what was claimed by Hieronymus? The machine was checked by several scientific personnel in Huntsville, Alabama as well as scientists in other parts of the world. It was nothing more than a radio frequency amplifier which had no radio frequency pickup (antenna) although it had a local oscillator to produce a radio frequency, and it had no output, only connections to the black plate. The machine, according to Hieronymus, amplified the eloptic energy along with the electrical signals, but this could not be verified.

Since no one could directly detect any eloptic signal, it was not possible to prove Hieronymus' claim. But did the machine work? Apparently sometimes, since the answers were at times correct. But was the machine picking up these psychic powers or was the person who touched the plates picking up the occult energy directly in his brain?

I saw the machine in operation and witnessed several correct diagnoses of people's physical condition, but I also witnessed either a failure of the machine or operator, or the machine was operated beyond its capability. I saw data of astronauts' physical condition taken by Hieronymus during a flight to the moon and the return, which did not agree with the data obtained by NASA Houston Control.

To obtain this data, Mrs. Hieronymus placed a picture of the astronauts in the receiver can and monitored the plate stickiness while reading the calibrated meter. Without knowing the actual feelings of the astronauts she reported her readings, a copy of which I obtained and compared with data from Houston. She was correct part of the time, but claimed to lose the signal when the astronauts went into the shadow of the moon, but she could read it while they were behind the moon.

The Hieronymus machine did not seem to improve accuracy in psychic reception but gave some operators enough confidence in themselves to gain knowledge from the universal storehouse of knowledge. It is possible that the machine actually tapped the psychic power which Hieronymus called eloptic energy, but it is more likely that the operator was directly receiving the spirit energy.

Another indication that it was not the machine but the operator actually receiving and directing the cosmic energy was given in the patent application on the Hieronymus machine. In the patent application, an experiment is described as follows: (from page 4 of the application)

"Such of the known elements as are required to feed growing plants have been transmitted to the plants through metallic conductors, as the plants were entirely isolated from the elements upon which they were fed. More precisely, seeds were planted in boxes in a darkened basement room. One of the boxes of plants containing some of the seeds was used as a control, and no apparatus for transmitting element radiations thereto were provided. The remaining boxes of plants had electrodes or plates of conducting material mounted or otherwise disposed adjacent thereto, and each box of plants was separately attached to a conductor extending to a point outside the building where electrodes or plates were attached to the conductors and allowed to remain exposed to the light. Such of the known elements as required to impart normal characteristics to the plants were apparently fed thereto by having the radiations of the elements from the light conducted to the plants through the wires and associated electrodes. The treated plants were relatively healthy but the control plant assumed the characteristics of growing vegetation which has been deprived of the elements in natural light. Particularly was the control plant devoid of chlorophyll while the remaining plants were green."

The plants staying green, while in the dark, could be a result of the experimenter receiving and transmitting to the plants that universal energy which may also be the source of our light and all matter in the universe.

The Theory of "Vol" and "Lovol"

Another trial at describing the cosmic force from which this physical universe originated, was attempted by Deane B. Caldwell at the 21st National Convention of the Astronomical League, meeting at Georgetown University in Washington, D.C. on July 4, 1967. Caldwell developed an amateur theory of the ultimate structure of the universe. He described "vol" as extremely tiny particles which are frictionless, perfectly elastic, and moving at the speed of light. These particles fill all of what is considered to be empty space. Each particle he calls a "vol," and collectively he calls the particles "lovol."

Caldwell thinks that we do not sense the lovol, but rather the three-dimensional whirlpools of lovol, which we call fundamental particles; i.e., atoms, electrons, protons, mesons, etc. He has the concept of a universe consisting of extremely small solid particles which are non-detectable, except when these particles take on a characteristic motion which can be detected as the solid material of our physical universe.

The source of the physical material in this world would be the non-detectables, vol and lovol; therefore, the energy source of this world would also be the non-detectables, vol and lovol.

Mr. Caldwell suggests that our galaxy, which is thicker near the axis of rotation than near the outer parameter, has such a shape because the lovol force holds the stars in position. He thinks that gravitational pull would cause the stars near the galaxy equator to fall toward the axis in much less time than the life of the galaxy (11.7 billion years). He also suggests that the earth has been maintained in its present orbit for 4.6 billion years by the lovol energy.

According to Caldwell's theory, every cubic foot of space contains enough material, lovol, to produce 1 cubic foot of any known material, such as gold, diamonds, platinum, etc., and he predicts that by the year 2,000, a machine will be changing lovol into any desired material or energy for the operation of space vehicles.

Caldwell certainly has a very fascinating idea, but what evidence do we actually have to support his theory? Apparently very little, except for the unusual stories told by the average layman who does not understand scientific laws. There are the stories of how God made this universe from that which is not visible; of the many vehicles which have been seen appearing and disappearing, traveling at unbelievable speeds, changing directions suddenly; of lights which have been observed moving through the sky for no apparent reason; of the many miracles which have happened; and of objects which move or can be moved with the mind. Yes, a theory like Caldwell's, as well as other theories of an unobstructed universe, would give substantiation to the strange and unusual events which have fascinated men for centuries.

From Lovol to Light via "Tachyons"

To build upon the theory of vol and lovol, the next step of these processes which has been observed many times is that light may be produced from the unknown universe. Apparently, the transition from the spiritual to the physical is light which is produced by the undetectable universe. But another step just prior to the generation of light has been theorized by Gerald Feinberg,[2] who calls this non-detectable particle a "tachyon."

He reports that the tachyon has not been detected, but the searching has not proven that it does not exist. Contrary to common belief, the tachyon is not inconsistent with the theory of relativity, which says that matter cannot exceed the velocity of light. In the case of the tachyon, it is imagined to come into existence already traveling faster than light. It has a strange behavior compared to ordinary particles; for, as the speed of the tachyon increases, the energy decreases. Moving at infinite speed, its energy is zero. Even when passing through empty space, the tachyon continuously radiates photons (electromagnetic energy).

The tachyon, although an imaginary particle, could be the signal carrier for the universal communication network and a basic part of the psychic universe.

Feinberg considers the possibility that the tachyon does not interact with matter. "The possibility that tachyons exist but do not interact at all with ordinary particles need not concern us, because if they do not interact with the objects that compose our measuring instruments, we have no possible way to detect them, and for our purposes, it is the same as if they do not exist at all." This comment relates in a very interesting manner with Stewart White's concept of the *Unobstructed Universe.*

The tachyon, or a similar particle, would provide the necessary carrier for the universal network signal and would answer many questions about psychic and spiritual phenomena. With an understanding of its function, we could establish a hookup with the universal communication network and make a giant leap in technological progress. The tachyons, as particles which produce light, fit many spiritual concepts that this physical world came from a spiritual world.

To formulate a theory of non-detectable particles, called tachyons, is not unreasonable, because, in physics many such particles have been suggested by scientists prior to their discovery. One of the most recent such particles is the evasive "neutrino,"

---

[2]Feinberg, Gerald, "Particles that Go Faster Than Light," *Scientific American*, Feb., 1970.

which for many years was only theorized to exist, but it has now been proven to exist.

The neutrino is similar to the vol and tachyon because it is a relativistic particle of extremely low mass and interacts only slightly with matter of the physical universe. The neutrino, billions of which constantly arrive at the earth from the sun, can pass completely through the earth without hitting–interacting with–the nuclear particles in the earth. The evasive neutrino is the closest detectable particle to the tachyon and vol, which implies that even more evasive particles are theoretically possible.

The Kundaline Phenomenon

A most unusual concept of how to tap cosmic power is proposed by Gopi Krishna,[3] a man from the mysterious land of India. He feels that mankind is evolving to a state such that extraordinary occult talents will be the normal adornment of the future man. He theorizes that the body contains a Fabulous Power Reservoir which has been tapped by the mystics, prophets, psychics, and divine healers. Even though much is known about the biological reactions of the human body, many mysteries continue to puzzle the learned, who would be amazed that a measure of evolution as a subtle process is at work in the average human body. This process may result in the formation of a bio-chemical essence of a volatile nature that can readily be transformed into a psychic radiation of high potency, according to Krishna. He thinks that the human body has the ability to manufacture a subtle, yet powerful substance which cannot be detected with any of the present methods of examination, but in the form of an "igmatic radiation," it can raise the human consciousness to a high level of awareness where other planes of existence with powerful forces are available.

This phenomenon of raising the human awareness is called Kundaline by Krishna, who considers it to be entirely biological in nature. With the awakening of Kundaline, an exciting activity begins throughout the entire nervous system, from the top of the brain to the tips of the toes; a sensation of an electrical charge

---

[3]Krishna, Gopi, *Biological Basis of Religion and Genius,* NC Press, Inc., New York, 1971.

runs through the body. Krishna believes that the powerful biological force floods the reproductive organs, which become abnormally active as if to keep pace with the activity of the entire nervous system. This radiant force illuminates the brain as it streams into it, courses through the nervous system, and stimulates all vital organs, especially the digestive system, adjusting it to the new life force introduced in the system.

As I obtained the ideas which were presented in *Cosmic Mysteries,* I experienced the feeling which Krishna described as Kundaline, except that no stimulation to the reproductive organs was noticed. In fact the thrill of communication with God so far surpassed all normal physical drives or urges that I lost all interest in the normal physical desires. My continuing desire was to maintain my communication with God, except at times when the electrically charged feeling became so strong that I had to reduce the contact to regain my contact with this physical existence. I felt as if too much power was entering my body for me to continue to receive it. I was overpowered by this cosmic awareness of our universe.

As is suggested by Krishna, there is apparently some connection between Kundaline and sexual thrills; however, I think that Kundaline is a stronger drive than sex, with a similarity between the physical feeling of the Kundaline thrill and the sexual thrill. Certainly this idea is not new but has been observed and commented upon by psychics, mystics, prophets, and many others for thousands of years. So often religious worship of God or gods is mixed with sexual activities. Probably the more famous example to Bible students was Baal worship involving the use of prostitutes in the temples.

When the powerful biological fluid is aroused, Krishna proposes that the reproductive fluid is sucked up through the spinal canal to irrigate and feed the various nerve junctions and the brain. This tonic food, in rich abundance, reaches every part of the brain, nourishing the brain cells and nerve fibers, stimulating them to a keen cosmic awareness. He thinks that the human brain is not fed by blood alone, but he proposes that the brain is nourished with psychic energy supplied by a limited number of nerves which extract the fuel from various parts of the body. Upon awakening Kundaline, he says that the entire nervous system is accelerated to a high degree of awareness by that powerful fuel, in the form of radiation which streams to the brain, enhancing its activity to such a degree that a highly extended consciousness results, which has such an overwhelming effect on the initiate that he is wafted to higher levels of existence where cosmic forces are available for his purposes. And with this change occurring in the subject's consciousness, which cannot be imagined by one who had not had this experience, the subject has a feeling of beholding a super-being, God, angels, etc. As cosmic consciousness is attained, Krishna feels that the subject believes he is communicating with the Creator, who reveals to him secrets of the universe and gives him the psychic powers of a super-human. Krishna very accurately expresses the feeling experienced by the writer and many others who have been thrilled by contacts with the cosmic power of our universe.

Kundaline is another name for the psychic power which is available and has been experienced by many people. It is available from the cosmic power center for those who meet the requirements for its use in the physical universe. However, Kundaline may be only a weak triggering energy which actually releases the powers of vol, P-K, orgone, eloptic, or the unknown cosmic powers which have apparently been observed in action by many people.

Possible Evidence of Psychic Energy

There are many strange, unexplained, paranormal sightings of lights and vehicles usually called UFO's which may actually be evidence of psychic energy going from the psychic universe into the physical universe. What causes this to happen and how it can be controlled by us is a matter that may have answers which can be found through research.

Because so many unusual, unidentified objects have been reported, there is evidence which should arouse us to an awareness of a natural phenomenon which requires an explanation. To obtain the answers, we could take two possible approaches—a better contact with higher life of the universe, or development of equipment which can tune in to the psychic realm.

The strange case of the man with a psychic leg was reported by Long John Nebel,[4] a radio, late-show entertainer. In his book, about many strange happenings which cannot be explained by reason, science, or the known laws of cause and effect, Nebel reports that a very specific demonstration of psychic power took place on his late-night radio show.

Oh his show, which covers about 35 stations, Nebel has probably interviewed about every unusual, peculiar, and psychic person who is known today. He has interviewed Jeanne Dixon, the late Bishop James Pike, Hugh Lynn Cayce, Arthur Ford, and Frank Edwards. He has witnessed several strange indications of cosmic powers on his shows, one of which was the unusual case of a man who could materialize a psychic leg to replace his missing physical leg.

Late one night, Nebel received a call from a man who said that he had lost one leg in an auto accident and had to walk on crutches, but at times he could produce a psychic leg and walk on it. This was probably one of the most unusual and unbelievable stories Nebel had heard, and he had heard many in his years with the late show.

Nebel asked him to come to his radio show and demonstrate his occult ability. The man came, but even though he tried diligently to produce the psychic leg, he was unable to achieve it and finally gave up. Nebel helped him over to a couch and continued with his radio show.

About 30 minutes later, the man left without his crutches, walking as if he had two normal physical legs, although only one was visible. He had tapped the psychic power sufficiently for the occult forces to support him as he walked.

Even though he utilized unknown powers to walk on an invisible leg, he was probably utilizing natural physical laws which are as yet not understood nor detected by the scientific community. He could have supported himself with controlled movement of molecules in his leg stump and/or the air directly below the stump. Like most psychic controls, he could not perform this feat

[4]Nebel and Teller, *The Psychic World Around Us,* Hawthorn, 1970.

continuously for some unknown reason. Even if he controlled the movement of molecules, the mysterious signal which controls the release of photons from the molecules to move them has never been detected.

Triggering Energy Is Minute

The search for the missing link between the release of photons from an object which is moved by psycho-kinesis and the brain is of primary interest to the scientifically minded. If the search results in an understanding of how and what that signal is, then we expect to be able to control objects with our mind more readily.

From a knowledge of how photons are released from matter, we see that the energy to release a photon is apparently very minute, but the triggering mechanism is not known. To illustrate how infinitesimal the triggering energy may be, consider how a human moves the largest object he can control. That object may be a ship, space vehicle, a modern nuclear power plant, an airplane, a multi-ton crane, or an automobile.

Considering the automobile, which is a common device that we move at will, let us trace through from the rear tires on the road to our minds and identify the triggering forces which cause the car to move.

The back wheels have molecules in their tires which strike or push against the molecules in the road to move the car. The wheels move from the power of the engine which receives its power from the burning mixture of gasoline and oxygen. The fuel and oxygen received their energy from the sun, indirectly, possibly millions of years ago for the fuels, but maybe only a few days ago for the oxygen since it was produced by plants using the sun's energy. Thus the engine's power came from the sun whose power was traced back in previous material.

The automobile engine has other power sources or triggering forces required for it to run. It has an electrical spark to ignite the gasoline, and it has an operator who decides when it will run and how fast. Not associated with the engine is the steering of the car, also controlled by the driver.

The driver uses his muscles to guide the car where he wants it to go and at what speed. His muscles receive energy from the foods digested in his stomach, but the triggering signals which move the muscles are small electrical impulses from the brain.

The source of the small electrical signals from the brain are within the mysterious depths of the brain which receives stimulation from the five senses. The source of the particular signals which cause the driver to control the car as desired is a mystery whose solution, some people speculate, is in understanding the origin of human intelligence. This source may have originated with the first Homo sapiens on this planet. However, proceeding further back, tracing to the next trigger source would take us to lower forms of life, then no life, then the sun again. All of which doesn't give a satisfactory explanation as to the source of the signal which controls the automobile.

Possibly the brain is an open-loop control system which receives its information through the five senses, assimilates it, and produces an electrical output signal to the muscles. As the muscles move, a signal is fed back to the brain; as the car responds, the eyes see and the signals again feed back into the brain to control muscles. But again, we ask what set the brain in motion originally? And where does it receive the new ideas? Chance? Not entirely, since there is so much evidence that signals do come to the brain through that mysterious sixth sense.

One such mysterious triggering signal was apparently received by the writer on his way to work. This undetectably weak signal which he was not consciously aware of seemed to control him as he approached school children standing beside a county road waiting for the school bus.

I had traveled this same road hundreds of times and the same children were in the usual place waiting for their bus. Usually I traveled along the open road at about 50 mph since there were only farms along it. But for some unknown reason, one morning I began slowing down at a very normal rate as I approached a family of children beside the road. I continued slowing although there was nothing in the way–I was not even aware that I was slowing down until the car was only moving about 10 mph.

Then without warning, one of the children, with his back to

me, jumped into the road directly in front of the car. As if my subconscious had known all along what was going to happen, I stopped the car completely about 10 feet from the child. As he turned and saw the car so close, he froze with fright and could not move for a moment, then he jumped back out of the road, and I, very much shaken, continued to work, considering how children must have a guardian angel.

As I drove, not thinking about what was logical, reasonable, or safe, some triggering signal was hitting my brain and causing the release of electrical signals to my muscles. That triggering signal may have released photons in my brain, which in turn generated the normal brain signals to the muscles.

As is the case with many people who have felt that God has spoken to them, my experience that morning added evidence that we have a sixth sense which receives some weak triggering signal from a universal intelligence. That triggering energy may be minute in the physical world, but the energy source in the physical world can supply power to move mountains, or move space vehicles to other parts of our universe.

He Made a Million

Arthur Stilwell, a well-known millionaire, experienced a special form of psycho-kinesis which moved him to build railroads. He progressed from a $40-a-week clerk to one of the wealthiest men of his day.[5]

Like most young couples, Arthur Stilwell and his bride began their married life with little more than bright dreams of the future. He had finished high school, but had no money, and his potential for wealth seemed to be very poor.

Many times during his youth, he had the feeling of voices in his mind. He would hear them when asleep or while sitting quietly, absorbed in an interesting book. This strange, new experience of cosmic forces at first frightened him, for Stilwell had been hearing these preternatural voices since he was 15. Sometimes he heard a distinct message, while at other times it seemed like some occult power was moving him. When still a young man he recorded in his

---

[5]Edwards, Frank, *Stranger Than Science,* Ace Books, Inc., New York, N.Y. 1959.

diary that he would marry a girl named Genevieve Wood within four years. He didn't know a girl with that name when the voice spoke to him. This correct prediction gave Arthur Stilwell confidence in the wisdom of the voices, but he never talked about them except to his wife, for fear that people would think him peculiar.

Time after time as he worked at his clerk's desk, the persistent force urged him to move West and build railroads for the expansion of the Western United States. After much pressure by the occult forces, Arthur left his job, and he and his wife packed their meager possessions in a borrowed wagon and started for Kansas City.

There he obtained a job in a bond house and brokerage firm, while keeping his eyes and ears open, heeding again and again the insistent voices who urged him to construct railroads.

With this cosmic power, Stilwell built railroads. He was considered a safe risk, and loans were available; he quietly bought the property and assembled the capital. To the surprise of many big railroad financiers, he soon had the Kansas City Belt Line Railroad in productive operation.

Stilwell did not understand how he knew the name of his wife four years before he met her, nor did he fathom the infallible advice that had taken him from a penniless clerk to a millionaire railroad builder in seven years. Nor did he see a logical reason to follow the bidding of the cosmic force which urged him to turn his railroad away from Galveston and terminate it in a saltwater swamp. But he did and amassed a fortune.

He built seven railroads, the Port Arthur ship canal, 40 cities and towns, two of which were named after him—Port Arthur, Texas, and Stilwell, Oklahoma. By following the psychic force, he amassed a fantastic fortune during his happy, fruitful career. With such forces directing him, everything he touched turned to money.

Other accomplishments of his life were the writing and publishing of 30 books, 19 of which were novels, including *The Light That Never Failed,* a longtime best seller. He even wrote a book in 1910 which prophesied in detail the coming of World War I.

Then in 1914 he wrote another preternatural book entitled, *To All the World Except Germany,* in which he told of the defeat of Germany and her allies, the independence of Finland and Poland, and the return of Palestine to the Jews.

Arthur Stilwell experienced a form of psycho-kinesis which was a weak signal force to his brain. This psycho-kinesis, causing the movement of his body, brought him wealth, fame, and happiness as he manipulated the mysterious cosmic powers.

5. MORE EVIDENCES OF COSMIC POWER

Some mysterious psychic trigger releases the photons from objects so that these small light bullets cause a recoil in the molecule, which moves the molecule in the opposite direction. Certainly much is unknown about the psychic trigger. Even its existence is speculation, but there is considerable evidence[1] that some undefined power is available to move objects.

The Moving Force for Molecules Is the Photon

All matter is continually releasing and absorbing photons. Matter receives the photons from all directions and releases them

---

[1] Backster, Cleve, "Evidences of a Primary Perception in Plants," *International Journal of Parapsychology,* Vol. X, 1968, No. 4.

Eisenbud, Jule, *The World of Ted Serios,* William Morrow and Co., Inc., 1967.

Schmidt, Helmut, "New Correlation Between a Human Subject and a Quantum Mechanical Number Generator," Docu. No. 01-82-0884, The Boeing Co., Seattle, Wash., 1967.

in all directions under normal conditions. Matter also receives and emits photons of a frequency primarily depending upon the temperature of the matter.

A hot object like the sun releases photons primarily in the visible frequency spectrum, while cold objects like the earth release photons which are not visible. But all objects are constantly absorbing and releasing photons.

If all photons being emitted from an object departed in one direction only, their recoil energy would kick the object in the opposite direction. Possibly photons can be triggered by the psychic signal to leave in a desired direction, thus accounting for the mysterious movement of objects in the psychic field. As photons are continuously absorbed from all directions and emitted in only one direction, the normal energy the objects receive from thermal radiation is used to move the object. Possibly not actual energy from the spirit universe is required to aid in moving the object, although apparently that energy is available. In fact many accounts of strange lights are indications that psychic energy is being transferred from the spirit world to this physical world.

How the photons can be released in a desired direction seems far beyond our present capability to understand, since scientists cannot tell the position of an electron in its orbit and the direction that the departing photon will take. But a description of how the unobstructed universe may function can help in exploring how the position of the electrons can be determined.

The spirit universe may be a system which completely permeates all of what we term space and matter. The spirit universe is material which is non-detectable in the physical world because it has no contact with the physical world, except when this psychic material is converted to light. This light may then be detected in the physical world. Objects in the spirit universe are spread out to fill the entire universe much like gas would fill a container in this universe. To illustrate, let us assume that one atom in the physical world is converted into light which can then be changed into the psychic material. When it becomes psychic material, it is incredibly spread throughout the entire psychic and physical universe.

To reverse the process and return the psychic atom, (which is not an atom but the information or identity of an atom) to this physical universe, requires the collecting of all of the atom's psychic material spread throughout the entire psychic universe into a point in the physical universe.

Another illustration is what happens to the soul of a person who dies. When the person dies, his identity which is fully recorded in the universal psychic realm, is spread throughout the entire universe. As the identity of the person (soul) is disconnected from the physical body, the soul enters the psychic universe and is immediately throughout the physical and psychic universe.

To reverse this process, the soul or identity of the person who died would have to be collected from throughout the psychic and physical universe to a point, to become the physical person again. When the soul comes back into the physical world, the first evidence may be the light outline of the person which is called a ghost. Possibly the light could be converted into the physical body of the person to reconstruct it, but probably much energy would be required, equivalent to the total energy required for an initially fertilized egg to become a full-grown adult.

There are many reported cases of people seeing the image of a person who has died. In some cases, more than one person sees the departed person's ghost at the same time, indicating that an actual image radiating light is present. In some cases, in addition to the ghost being seen, there are evidences that the spirit being can move objects as illustrated in the extremely unusual story of the Griggs' ghost in Madison, Alabama.

This story of a mother who knew that she was going to die, made preparations for her death, but most amazing of all, returned from the dead to convince her husband of a spiritual existence, was related to the author by the husband, Jerry. The story has been verified by others who also saw and spoke to Mrs. Griggs after her death.

A Mother Aided Her Family from the Spirit World

Although not entirely a story of psycho-kinesis, the extremely interesting case of the Jerry Griggs family of Madison, Alabama contains several specific instances where objects were moved by a discarnate spirit.

Jerry and his wife, Lorie, were a happy couple with two young children in the 1960's with no hint that tragedy was about to strike. Lorie was a devout Catholic girl, but Jerry had little interest in religious matters. For no apparent reason, since Lorie was in perfect health, she told Jerry that they should prepare for her death by moving closer to her parents so they could help with the children. Jerry saw no reason to entertain such an unpleasant idea, but it wasn't long before, strangely enough, one of the neighbors of her parents offered to sell them their house. Jerry accepted the offer, and they moved to Madison from Decatur, Alabama.

Shortly after they moved, with no prior warning, Lorie died suddenly of a cerebral hemorrhage.

Not long after her death, Jerry and the children had been to a drive-in eating place where the car had become littered with cups, paper, potato chips, etc. Shortly after parking the car in the driveway and entering the house, Monica, the younger daughter (about seven), said she saw her mother sitting in the front seat of the car. Monica described her mother in detail, including bracelets, her dress, and a rosary which Lorie had been wearing when she was buried. Monica had not seen them on her mother after her death, since she had not been allowed to view her mother's body.

Monica said her mother was smiling and extremely beautiful with glistening white teeth. When Lorie started to open the car door to get out, Monica noticed that her foot went through the door before she opened it. Monica also saw her mother at the kitchen window smiling at her.

When Jerry went to the car to investigate, he did not see his wife, but he was amazed to discover that the front side of the car and seat, where Monica had seen Lorie, was spotless, although it had only been a minute or two since they had left the car in a mess.

From the spirit world, apparently Lorie was able to clear up debris in the physical world, which agrees with the theory that a signal exists that can release photons from matter in a manner that can move objects or produce desired changes.

After Lorie's first appearance to Monica, she was seen by Jerry in visions and dreams and she talked to Jerrie Jean, the oldest child. Jerrie Jean would often request that Lorie come to Jerry in his dreams, and Jerry would have a vivid dream of being with Lorie and talking with her.

In the dreams, Lorie told Jerry much about this spirit world where she was very busy and happy. She missed him and the children, and she was returning to help them adjust to her absence, but primarily she was concerned that Jerry did not believe in the spiritual world. She encouraged him to study more about the spiritual aspects of the universe.

Another unusual way that Lorie communicated with Jerry was through a medium; Lorie would tell the medium many things about Jerry and the children, which the medium would tell Jerry. Lorie said she was using these methods to convince Jerry that there is a spiritual existence and he should prepare for it.

Jerry was extremely happy with the dream visits from his wife, but he still lived in the physical world and Lorie lived in the spirit world. He had work here and she had work there, according to her explanation of what she was doing.

Finally, in a beautiful farewell dream, she said that she was needed more in the spirit world, that Jerry and the children had adjusted to her departure, and she would not be returning again to visit with them.

This amazing story has been written down in detail by Jerry, who expects to publish his family's experiences in communicating with the spirit world.

Because Lorie was seen by several people at the same time is evidence that she was able to produce an image of herself in the physical world by generating photons, using some spiritual medium. Since most of Lorie's communication with Jerry was in dreams, there is an indication that the spiritual signal released energy in his brain to produce the dream visions.

Lorie may have produced the visions and conversation in Jerry's subconscious mind by means of the psychic signal supernaturally releasing photons within Jerry's brain to produce the apparent words and images which he experienced.

Several incidents in the psychic experiences of Jerry and his two children indicate that there is a psychic force available from the psychic universe. These incidents are: the image of Lorie or light which is energy; the cleaning up of the front area of the car; and the communication with Jerry in dreams.

Another case of a departed loved one being seen was related to this writer by Gloria, who is a friend of the family. She has had several striking psychic experiences, one of which occurred when she was a young girl, six years old.

Gloria had a dearly loved aunt who died when Gloria had very little understanding of death. Several days after her aunt's funeral, she was returning to the house with a bucket of water when she saw her aunt! As Gloria was approaching the front porch of their house, she saw an image of her dead aunt crouched beneath the porch. Her aunt had on a dress which Gloria had seen her wearing before her death. Gloria saw her image for only a moment before she disappeared. Gloria said nothing about what she saw, nor did her grandmother, who was with her, mention seeing the image.

The fact that her grandmother did not see the image is an indication that the psychic image was impressed directly on Gloria's brain by the departed spirit of her aunt and was not caused by a release of photons from the air under the porch. There is a possibility that the grandmother did see the image but did not want to say anything to frighten her young granddaughter.

The Link of Light Between Psychic and Physical

As material of the psychic world is converted into light, it enters the physical. The psychic material may be converted to light in the physical image of a deceased person, or the psychic material may appear as just a light.

So many mysterious, unusual lights have been seen which seem to be a linking of the psychic and material worlds, that the converting of psychic material to physical material may be a normal part of the overall universal cycle of matter, biological life, and spirits. Possibly the psychic material is constantly being changed to light throughout the universe.

On a seemingly uneventful Sunday morning, Oct. 31, 1971, about 10 a.m., a man looking at the windows of the Mount Olive Baptist Church, Brunswick, Georgia, was amazed to see a cross of light in the windows. Such a cross had not been noticed before. After he brought the cross of light to the pastor's attention, they tried to determine the source of the cross. All that could be ascertained was that when a light of any magnitude, such as a match, flashlight, or light bulb was on in a room of the church, the cross appeared in the window.

The cross could also be seen from inside looking out. The light cross was of sufficient magnitude for a camera to take a picture of it, which was printed in many newspapers.

The pastor, Rev. Walter L. Handerson, said that soon after the cross appeared in his church, other churches in the area also reported preternatural crosses of light in their windows.

Eye-Witness Accounts of Strange Lights

In 1954, Walter Jackson, who is now a NASA space vehicle project engineer and a friend of the writer, was stationed in Tokyo. As a member of the Air Force, he was a tower operator at the Tokyo Airport. He had no interest in UFO's. One night something happened which caused him to give some serious consideration to a very strange phenomenon of this earth. While he was controlling aircraft, he sighted a light several miles away. The light did not appear to be a normal airplane light because it was not flashing on and off nor moving at all. As he looked more closely in the direction of the light, he could vaguely see the outline of a vehicle. He drew a picture of this craft on the blackboard for me, and it had the typical saucer shape of a UFO. Since there were fighter aircraft in the area at that time, he vectored two of them toward the light. When they were within radar range of the light, both aircraft pilots reported picking up a radar contact, and they said that they were intercepting it. As they approached the UFO, they were unable to see it, although they were much closer than Jackson. They continued toward the radar target and flew through it! They did not see the craft although Jackson saw it from a distance. Both planes made a 180-degree turn back toward the target and picked it up again on radar—and again they flew through the target!

Another UFO was seen that same year, 1954, in the same area of the world. The person who reported this sighting to me did not know about Jackson's experience. A sailor, Ponder, was lying on the deck of a carrier one night off the coast of Korea. He was gazing at the heavens as we all enjoy doing. He noticed that one star exhibited a very strange behavior. It moved about in one area of the sky. At first he and the other sailors thought that it might possibly be some enemy aircraft, but why would the enemy have a light showing? They notified the Officer of the Deck of the strange light. He asked the radar operators to check, but nothing was observed on radar. A few nights after this incident, the crew was again on the deck of the ship and they saw a vivid red light near the horizon. This light moved up and down and from right to left. It could have been a port running light of a ship, yet the ships were not supposed to turn on running lights since they were operating under battle conditions. Again this peculiar light was checked by radar but could not be detected. No contact! This time the crew didn't bother to tell the Officer of the Deck about the light.

In the Cape Kennedy, Florida, area in 1967, an unusual light was seen by Don Sonnamaker, a friend of the writer. He was working the night shift at the *Saturn* launch stand and noticed a bright light directly above the test stand. He watched the light for five to ten minutes, but it had no motion whatsoever. It was much brighter than the stars in the sky. In fact, it was as bright or even brighter than the floodlights located on the gantry. Finally, he had to cease watching and go inside to perform a task. Some time later when he came outside to check the light, it was gone.

A few weeks later the Sonnamaker children, along with other school children, were returning home from school one afternoon when they noticed a white object, stationary in the sky, not much more than 1,000 feet above the trees. (The altitude was later determined by asking several of the school children where the object was located, and since the children were spread out over a considerable area, by triangulation a reasonable estimate of the altitude could be determined.) All of the children reported seeing the same object, a disc shape with a white surface. They described the surface as having the appearance of an egg shell. The children watched the object for several minutes as they walked toward home. The object did not move at all. Later when they looked for the object, it was no longer there.

Another UFO sighting which appears somewhat like this egg-shaped object was reported over Castle Rock, Colorado in the same year. The sheriff's deputy, Werner, said that some one dozen or so residents or reliable citizens, reported seeing a big unidentified flying bubble over the town. One individual said he saw the bubble hovering about 50 feet over him with about a dozen lights, all the color of car headlights, and they were shining on him. He said it was transparent but solid. As they watched the object, it hovered for some time over the Douglas County Courthouse, but finally shot straight up and disappeared after shooting out a couple of balls of fire.

These are only a few of thousands of similar phenomena where people have observed objects which cannot be explained. Of course, in all cases, it is just a statement of individuals that they have seen something; and, undoubtedly, something is there, or normally truthful people become prevaricators when discussing UFO's. What are these objects? They may be natural or some artificially manufactured device. They could be natural objects which we are not aware exist at this time. It seems particularly strange that the UFO observed by Jackson near Tokyo could be seen as a physical light, and was picked up on radar but could not be seen by the pilots as they flew through the spot where Jackson saw the light. There are some very plausible explanations to these peculiar characteristics of UFO's. The object could have simply, quickly accelerated and left the spot where the radar contact had been, about the time the planes arrived. Or, the inability of the pilots to pick it up visually, may have been due to the object being at a lower altitude where the background was black or dark, thus not providing sufficient illumination to see the UFO. However, Walt Jackson could see it because he was looking from a darker area on the ground up into the lighter night sky. Another possibility is that these UFO's are nothing more than the light produced by psychic material being converted into light.

The Bright Light Messages

The many strange lights observed by many people from the beginning of history indicate that this is one means of communication used by higher life. These lights are mentioned in the Bible as the "burning bush," Paul's "conversion blinding light," "the cloven tongues of fire," and others. Since Biblical days bright lights have been involved in many messages to man; for example, the miracle of Fatima, and the many recent UFO lights reported. The lights that have been considered UFO's have caused many people to become aware of higher life and even question their relationship to God. Whether the lights were used to produce an understandable message for the observer or simply made him consider his relationship to God, they served as a means of higher intelligence contacting Homo sapiens.

Charles Fort[2] reported many occasions when unusual clouds, lights, etc. were associated with violent rainstorms. Possible explanations for the association are: the weather conditions cause the lights, such as ball lightning; the lights are controlled by higher intelligence trying to inform man of a coming event; the lights indirectly cause clouds to form; or the lights are in the "minds" of the observers, caused by group imagination or by signals from higher intelligence.

In California, where mystics, psychics, spiritualists, and other interesting idea-people have established a stronghold, Teska, a communicator, receives direct messages from the "Celestial High Command" and sends the messages, to those interested, in a publication, *The White Star.* Teska claims to have seen the UFO's of the higher life while she talked with them.[3] Although Teska does not see a bright light while communicating, she uses expressions of "light" very much in the bulletins.

On September 6, 1970, strange bright lights were seen over Decatur, Alabama, and Dennis W. Billings obtained a picture of them. The lights were low, but Billings heard no sound and they were not normal aircraft navigational lights. Although possibly unassociated with the bright lights, Hans Hueter, a German rocket scientist working for NASA in Huntsville, Alabama died on September 6, 1970 a few hours before the lights were seen. Are many of the UFO bright lights the spirits of departed souls and/or other spirits coming in to pick up and take away another spirit? (When Jesus, after he ascended, appeared to Paul on the road to Damascus, he appeared as a bright light which blinded Paul.)

---

[2]Fort, Charles, *The Book of the Damned,* Holt, Rinehart and Winston, Inc., New York, N.Y., 1941.

[3]*The White Star Illuminator,* Volume 1, No. 2., Jan.-Feb., 1958.

Walker's Light

During the last week of March 1970, at least three unusual lights were seen in the Huntsville, Alabama area. The first one coming to the attention of the writer was reported by a ten-year-old boy who was looking at the stars through his small telescope. He saw one star moving relative to another. The moving star moved in toward, away from, and around the stationary one. The next unusual light was reported by the Huntsville and Decatur police. This was a bright light which slowly drifted across the sky and faded out about 5:10 a.m. It was seen by several police over a 35-minute period. They could have seen Comet Bennett, but their description did not fit.

The third unusual light was by far the most fantastic. This light was seen by Jerry Walker and his wife Jo on Easter morning, March 29, 1970 for nearly two hours.

Jerry and Jo delivered papers in Tennessee northeast of Huntsville, Alabama. Neither Jerry nor Jo were known by the writer until after this fateful morning. However, Jerry has a sister who is a close friend of the author and his family, and she is willing to vouch for the high integrity of Jerry and Jo.

On this soon to become a frightful morning, Jerry and Jo were running about 30 minutes late with their delivery of the morning paper for the *Huntsville Times.* It was a cool damp morning after rains during the night, and the sky was forebodingly overcast as Jerry and Jo began their paper route.

After delivering several papers, Jo became aware of a strange light in the sky. At first, she assumed it to be an airplane, but it did not behave nor look right for an airplane. The light was not blinking and it had a bright, white appearance; but, most mysterious of all, it seemed to follow them. It was also coming closer. As it came closer, it appeared larger and brighter, until it was so bright that it could not be looked at directly and it lighted up the countryside.

Jerry had the impression that it was coming down on top of his car. So he stopped and backed up to move away from the point toward which it was headed. As the mysterious, brilliant light descended to the road surface about 500 feet ahead of the car, Jo thought she saw three legs extended below the light.

She said, "It looked like the 'thing' landing on the moon!"

But as soon as it touched the road, it began to rise again, picking up speed rapidly. It accelerated to an unbelievable speed and was soon a small light in the sky. During the entire spectacular episode, it made no sound at all.

Jerry and Jo, although severely shaken, continued their paper route with the light continuing to pace them at a great distance. They had the very eerie feeling that they were being watched by alien beings.

The light they saw apparently had no connection with the Comet Bennett since it was cloudy.

If we wanted to speculate on what the light was, using some imagination, we would say that it was a space vehicle with passengers observing Jerry and Jo. The passenger spacemen came in for a closer look, but realizing that the vehicle (car) they were following contained intelligent beings whom they had no wish to frighten further or communicate with, they aborted their landing just as they touched down, in the same manner as the *Apollo* moon lander can take off again from the moon just after a touchdown.

Other factors related to this incident may give further clues of what happened. Jo and Jerry had attended the funeral of Jo's uncle the day before. She had the feeling of seeing her departed father several times as she looked at the body of her dead uncle. Jerry had had a 19-year-old friend killed at the exact same spot that the light touched down about a year before. Jerry's side of the family has a history of visions, ghosts, and other unexplained visual phenomena, although Jerry had no previous experience of seeing unexplained sights. It was Easter morning and probably both had heard many times the Easter story of an angel descending from heaven and rolling the stone away from the tomb of Jesus. "His countenance was like lightning, and his raiment white as snow." *(Matt. 28:3)* A late show on TV for that night was science fiction about a UFO landing on top of a car, and, although they had not watched the show, they had probably seen the advertisements of it. Another possibly related factor was that relatives were praying for Jerry and Jo to turn to God and follow Christ's way of life. This interesting combination of factors could have caused a psychological reaction in the couple.

During the fateful early morning hours, the clouds could have parted enough for them to see Comet Bennett. This stimulus could have set off a chain reaction in the imagination of the couple.

Their emotionally disturbed condition due to recalling the death of Jo's uncle and Jerry's friend and subconscious memories could have caused them to suspect that the light was following them. This fear that they were being followed would have further stimulated them to think that the light came very close and even descended (as in the Bible) to the road in front of them. Both of them having the same experience is not unusual since several cases are available where trapped miners and others shared common thoughts. This is particularly true if they talk about what they are seeing. Each one tends to adjust mentally to see what the others describe.

This psychological concept of what happened was discussed with a psychology professor at the University of Alabama. He also suggested such an explanation.

Considering the religious implications, regardless of what happened, whether a joint illusion or an alien craft landing, or the real thing, the incident brought many people's attention to God. From this viewpoint, the least that can be said is that some people had an encounter with a universal being.

Throughout the Bible many stories are told of light, men, angels, clouds, flaming chariots, etc. accosting men and directing their attention to God. Maybe God still uses psychological and physical occurrences to bring attention to himself and cause people to turn from their selfish way of living to the Christ way of possible universal living.

Lights Associated with Death

My father tells the story of a globe of light being seen near a person who had died. This occurred in a house which was lit by kerosene lamps during the night while relatives were sitting up with the body. The globe of light hung near the deceased person for a while then slowly floated away.

This strange type of story is repeated many times by Myers[4]

---

[4]Myers, F. W. H., *Human Personality and Its Survival of Bodily Death*, University Books, Inc., New Hyde Park, New York, 1961.

and others who have investigated the existence of the soul. The typical story is that after the person dies, a dim glow of light is sometimes seen (and photographed) above the person's head. The globe is attached to the head by a thin thread which becomes thinner as the globe of light floats higher, and it finally breaks as the globe floats away. The globe of light is considered to be the soul by some observers.

As the physical being's personality passes from this physical world into the spiritual world, there may be a path involving the thin thread of light and the globe of light. We could speculate that the personality travels into the spirit world via the path of light, and when the light disappears he is in the spirit realm. If the spirit returns to the physical world, he can return via the path of light. It is not truly a path but evidence that psychic material is being converted into physical material.

Not all departing souls have such a peacefully quiet globe of light attached to them, because the relative of a friend of the writer saw a very bright, fast-moving ball of light the day before one of her relatives died.

One evening about sundown three of her relatives were sitting on their front porch in peaceful Paint Rock Valley, Alabama when they saw a bright fireball come rolling rapidly down the mountainside toward the porch of the house in which they lived. They said the fireball seemed to explode near the porch, but upon examining the area where the flash occurred, they could find no damage or traces of fire and residue from the fireball.

The day after the strange fireball was seen, a member of this family who saw the fireball shot and killed himself on the exact spot where the fireball exploded.

This strange occurrence could be explained by assuming that the psychic beings knew of the impending death and reacted to it by producing the fireball.

Tennessee Lights

A weird, unexplained light which moves down a railroad track (without the train) is a regular nightly puzzling event in Tennessee near the Alabama line just east of Fayetteville.

Although I have not seen this light, I have talked to people who have seen it many times. One of the natives of that area said that the light would appear at a distance down the railroad track, then seem to move toward the observer, becoming larger as the observer becomes more apprehensive.

No one has been able to approach near the elusive light, which will move away and disappear when you try to go near it.

There is nothing unusual associated with the light, but there is no explanation for it; therefore, it could be light from the spirit world.

Another much more dramatic light is a common occurrence in Sleepy Hollow, near Union City, Tennessee. This light was observed by David Bartholomew and two friends in February, 1970. He reported, "The first time I saw the light, it winked teasingly on and off. It flitted from one side of the road to another, grew a fierce, bloody red, and then faded out. Coming back as a gentle glow, it flipped over and over like a monkey by its tail."

What it is no one seems to know, but it appears on a secluded country road between Milan and Trenton in northwest Tennessee. It has been seen by many people who tell their tales since way back when. There are tales of several unexplained murders, floating pebbles, screams, and voices.

When Bartholomew and his two friends spent the night in Sleepy Hollow, they heard a scream and footsteps as if someone was taking giant steps on the twig-carpeted, pitch black forest floor.

After the initial, uncanny introduction to Sleepy Hollow, the three men drove back into town for more supplies and courage. When they returned, they saw a parked car at the top of the hollow, but no one was around it. They drove past it, then returned, and this time there was a woman in the car. They also saw the outline of a man on the far side of the car. When they stopped to offer help, the man replied in a gravelly voice, "You boys can camp here if you want. We don't care if you don't mind where you are!"

How this man knew that they intended to camp was a mystery, since only their parents had been told where they were going.

Bartholomew continues his tale in the *Union City Daily*

Messenger, "We parked our truck about halfway down the Hollow and waited. Then it came. We rushed the light but it disappeared. There are several outbuildings nearby, and we searched them with a fine-tooth comb but found nothing but rotten boards and discarded trash.

"On one occasion, we thought there was a car approaching from the opposite direction. It was the light, which grew red and then faded away.

"We returned to the camp about midnight and were just crawling into our sleeping bags when it sounded as if we were in the midst of an elephant stampede. Then, we heard human voices, though unintelligible, from the depths of the Hollow. Suddenly, shooting broke out.

"We flattened ourselves on the tent floor and held our own weapons ready for anything as a fusillade of semi-automatic fire sounded through the darkness that was dripping with excitement and fear at the same moment. Then some heavy pistol shots, once more the trampling sound, and then, thank goodness, silence.

"Gradually, calm and quiet began to reign. By 3 a.m. we were all asleep and serenity was king until we rose about 6 a.m., feeling more like men for having withstood the ordeal.

"I can still offer no explanation for the light, although I have viewed it several times since. When I told my story, I started a run on the area and more strange stories have arisen than you can shake a stick at.

"Some samples include cars that won't move up the hill from the Hollow while the light is on, objects floating around inside cars, rocks floating near car windows, voices, footsteps, and sudden temperature changes."

Bartholomew's tale certainly seems like a wild one, but apparently there must be validity to some of these stories of unexplainable lights and other weird movings of pebbles, rocks, etc. Why would stories of strange lights also include other strange phenomena?

When lights are seen, based upon known facts which are established by scientific research, we can assume that an energy source such as a chemical reaction is producing the light by heating atoms to an energy level where the photons being released are of a frequency visible to the eye. Light is also produced by an electrical energy source, such as a charged cloud, which produces lightning, or batteries, generators, etc., which supply energy to heat a wire filament or gas to a temperature where it will give off visible light. And light is produced in other less understood ways by a lightning bug or glow worm. This light is produced by a material which gives off visible light at an unusually low temperature.

Possibly there are other natural methods of producing light which would explain these unusual lights which do not have a detectable energy source. Why should some of these mysterious lights be seen time after time in the same location while others are seen only once? Some of the uncanny lights seem to fit a consistent, but inconceivably puzzling, pattern.

Flying Lights

An uncle of the writer said that he had often seen strange lights while flying across the western United States in his small private plane. He did not consider the lights frightening, only a mystery. He seldom saw these lights, and then he saw them only one at a time. Sometimes he flew his plane close to the lights, which were nothing but a disc-shaped light moving through the air, sometimes against the wind with a rippling motion. He felt that he could have flown his plane through the light and would have hit nothing.

Similar lights were seen by a NASA aeronautical engineer near Fort Payne, Alabama; however, these lights moved in a very systematic manner.

While the engineer and his wife were driving from Atlanta to Huntsville, Alabama one night, they saw four lights moving in formation, with one light either blinking on and off or moving quickly back and forth in the path of flight.

The four lights were first sighted when they were at a considerable distance, but they moved in much closer and descended toward their car as they drove along the road. These four strange lights came within a few hundred feet of the car, which the engineer and his wife had stopped so they could watch the lights better. When the lights were at their closest point of approach, they were estimated by the engineer to be 30 to 50 feet in diameter and moving at 50 to 100 mph. While near them, the four lights made a turn as they descended, then continued moving horizontally down an electrical high voltage power line, which could have been an energy source for the lights.

The engineer said one very unusual thing happened when the lights were near him. They maintained a triangular formation, with one light leading and two out to the sides and behind, while the fourth light blinked on and off or moved quickly back and forth in the direction of flight. He said that one time as the blinking light seemed to contact the forward light, both lights disappeared momentarily. Then the front light came on steadily, and the blinking light continued its peculiar behavior in the line of flight.

The lights were about the intensity of the full moon and were transparent. There were no vehicles of any sort visibly attached to or around them.

The Aeroengineer felt strongly that the lights were some unknown natural phenomenon, not a visiting vehicle from outer space.

Four lights were seen near Pulaski, Tennessee by many people, several of whom I talked to. These lights were first seen hanging vertically, completely stationary, in space. All were about the intensity of a full moon, and the top light was about the size of a full moon. The lower three lights, all equally spaced, were about one-half the diameter of the top light. After at least ten to 15 minutes, the lower three lights all began to move slowly toward the big light. They maintained the same spacing as if they were on a string being pulled into the big light. As each small light entered the large light, the small one could not be seen—and when the last one entered the top light, the large light mysteriously disappeared.

An energy source for all of these preternatural lights may be the psychic material which is being converted directly into visible light, or the psychic signal triggers the release of visible light in the earth's atmosphere. The energy source may be spiritual energy from the unobstructed universe. It may have intelligent guidance or it may follow some prescribed natural path. Even intelligent guidance could be a natural phenomenon. Some lights may be spirits entering the physical world to pick up those who are going into the spirit world, while some lights may be the vehicles or playthings of spirit beings who are traveling, playing, or performing some worthy function.

The lights, after entering the physical world, could also form an image of a person or a vehicle like a "Flying Saucer," since these evasive vehicles have been observed to appear and disappear, move at incredible speeds, turn at terrific rates, with no sound at all, as if they are only an image.

A possible explanation of UFO's is that they are only images projected into the physical world from the psychic world, whose purpose is exactly the purpose which they serve; i.e., to arouse people to consider life on other planets of the universe, higher intelligence, spirit beings, and communication with other worlds.

On Nov. 5, 1971 Laura and Allen Hayes were driving near Summerville, Georgia, about 50 miles from Fort Payne, Alabama, when Laura saw what appeared to be a shooting star which was first seen moving fast, as if it was coming from behind Mars. (Laura described Mars as the bright red star.)

The shooting star followed a slightly curved, nearly vertical path toward the earth until it was about halfway to the horizon, then it slowed down suddenly and gently floated down. Very strange behavior for a meteor! When the light was low on the horizon, they lost sight of it behind a hill. As they came out from behind the hill, the strange light was still there, but now it was going on and off slowly. It was now a large light, but diffused, as if it had a curtain in front of it, and it seemed to be divided into four sections because a cross shape through its middle was not as bright as the four quadrants. Then the light went behind the hill and they saw it no more.

When Laura saw the strange behavior of the light she thought about a "spaceship."

Allen doesn't believe in UFO's and he considered it to be just an odd light.

If there is an intelligence who controls the lights, what is the purpose of their strange behavior? They move, flash, and change shapes as if a child were playing with a flashlight.

If these lights are natural, their behavior does not seem to be any stranger than lightning flashes to a deaf man who had been blind. The lightning would run about at random for no apparent reason if he had no understanding of the nature of lightning.

So these mystifying lights may be an evidence of a natural conversion of psychic cosmic powers into physical energy in the physical universe.

The weird light seen by Laura and Allen which seemed to be like a window with four panes may have been a window into the elusive psychic world, which may be the source of all power.

Laura told me the story about the light they had seen, eight days after the sighting, at the time I had written this chapter to the point of their story. Since I had already developed a theory about how light is the link between the psychic and physical worlds, I felt that if an intelligence is trying to communicate with me, he certainly selected an appropriate way of saying to me, "Adrian, you have seen through the window into the spiritual world!"

If that is not the message but only a series of coincidences, with imagination tying them together, then an even greater mystery confronts us–the mind and events. Since I have had so many experiences throughout my life which seemed to be a higher intelligence communicating with me, I must assume again that I have received a message from the universal mind. This same psychological mystery confronted me while I received the ideas which were presented in *Cosmic Mysteries.*

I asked myself, "What if these ideas are just imagination?" I had asked God to give me information. Ideas came which could be answers from Him. I could have assumed that these ideas were pure imagination and not an answer to my questions and ignored the ideas. I would probably have stopped receiving ideas (answers) because I would not listen. I also question if I am being open minded or if I am trying to build an exciting concept with a vivid imagination. Since I have been writing this book, I have been asking the universal energy intelligence to help me understand psycho-kinesis. This is a subject about which I had no strong desire to write when I began, but now I find myself completely fascinated by the ideas, with apparent answers coming from the spiritual realm as I request information.

As I wrote this material, that feeling of a strong link-up with universal intelligence came again. The same feeling came over me strongly while I was obtaining the information in *Cosmic Mysteries.* It came late at night as I asked God questions and I received ideas which explained the Life Cycle of the Universe. It was again after midnight as I wrote these concepts, and I had the feeling that when I ask God questions, answers will be obtained. I do not feel that these answers are complete but only sufficient to elevate one to the next level of understanding.

I said, "Lord help me to see through that window into the spiritual universe!"

Spirit-Controlled, Light-Opened Doors

With that request, this chapter would have ended if another very convincing message had not also been conveyed to me in April, 1972. This story is additional evidence that the energy intelligence is readily available, providing us wisdom and power far beyond our most optimistic expectations.

In late April, 1972, while trying to locate a person sensitive to the spirits of discarnate beings, I contacted a friend who was psychic and requested that she go with us to investigate the famous Tennessee light that moves along above a railroad near Fayetteville.

The local story about this light was that a black railroad train conductor had been lynched shortly after the Civil War at the place where the light appeared. This story suggested that the light may be controlled from the spirit realm by the soul of the train conductor. In the hope of using a psychic to try to communicate with the discarnate spirit controlling the light, this friend had been asked to visit the famous eerie spot.

She could not go, but suggested another "sensitive" who was contacted, and she referred me to another person who was attuned to the spirit realm. This was how I learned about Barbara Beavers and her unusual, powerful occult abilities.

Barbara could not visit the Tennessee light location that night, but she did have a very specific message for me. Of many unusual experiences which she could have told me, she was directed to relate a true account of the specific reconfirmation of my idea about light being the key to the spirit universe.

In late October, 1971, at the time when I was requesting confirmation that light is the link between the physical and psychic universes, Barbara was visiting friends in Fort Lauderdale,

Florida. Late one night, she and two friends, who were nightclub entertainers, were seated on a bed discussing religious concepts, spirit energy, and generally brainstorming the concepts of higher cosmic consciousness. Barbara had followed the techniques for tapping cosmic powers which are presented in previous chapters. She had received a concept of God from a Baptist Church which she had attended until she reached a point of wanting to obtain a better contact with universal energy intelligence than could be obtained from the church. She realized that the God whom she knew in her spiritual mind was not the God of fear and punishment portrayed by well-meaning people in the church.

Barbara had left the church and continued to establish a stronger link with the universal intelligence. She was exercising this link in her daily life, and especially on that late October night when a definite message was received from universal intelligence for her, her two friends, and this writer whom she did not even know.

As the three psychically attuned people discussed the psychic philosophies of Paul Twitchell who had recently died, they were wondering if he had found the spirit world to be basically as he thought it would be. With Paul on their minds, a strange manifestation occurred before them.

Barbara noticed a light beginning to form at the junction of the ceiling and wall across from the bed. Because of her experiences with such apparitions, she said nothing to her friends about the light for fear of adversely affecting its activities, but almost by the time Barbara noticed the light forming, the man commented, "Look up in the corner and tell me what you see." Barbara replied, "Yes, I've been watching it." "Then you do see that light," he said.

Even though these three people were strongly attuned to the psychic realm, they were still awesomely reverent as this spirit manifestation became a reality of light and moved along the wall-ceiling line toward a bathroom door which was about 1 inch open, allowing the light from the bathroom to dimly light the bedroom. Since the light from the bathroom was brighter than the psychically controlled light which moved into it, when the moving light arrived in the bathroom doorway, the occult light could no longer be seen by the people, but they were aware of its psycho-kinetic power because the bathroom door flew fully open!

Not only did this force (represented by a light) open the bathroom door, but all inside doors in the house, even though some had been locked with a bolt! The strange force had performed its task so quietly that the people were unaware that other doors had opened until they left the bedroom where the strange light had appeared.

Their next shock, after the bathroom door flew open, was to find the bedroom door fully open, although it had been locked and even though it dragged heavily on the carpet as it was opened. But they heard no sound as it opened. They next noticed a child's bedroom door completely open, although it had been closed, but not locked. And as they continued checking doors throughout the house, some of which had been completely closed while others had been left ajar, they found all inside doors fully open. The outside doors were still closed.

As Barbara related this uncanny cosmic experience to me, that physical and mental sensation of contact with universal intelligence came over me. I remembered how I had asked for confirmation that light is the link to the psychic universe back in late October or early November. Now, some six months later, a person whom I had never met told me about a psycho-kinetic light opening doors in a house in Fort Lauderdale. As the strong sensation of cosmic awareness came over me, the message, "Light opens the doors to the spirit universe.", was impressed upon my mind.

With cosmic awareness so strong, I asked Barbara how she felt when elevated to the energy intelligence level.

She expressed her feelings as being transmuted with energy flowing into her so that she had no desire for food. She felt psychically elevated, swirling, accelerated, sharpened body feelings of well-being, crispness of thought, emphasized importance of living, a warm and calm sense of energy flowing into her body, and her mind seemed to function like a computer memory drum with preternatural information being seen and heard. She would have to write down the message before the "images" and "sounds" would cease and before the drum would continue on to another message.

Barbara did not feel a need to exercise psycho-kinesis although she was sure she could if she tried, but she felt that there were more rewarding uses of her psychic powers.

Many other stories of psychic lights substantiating the ideas presented in this chapter will probably come to the writer's attention, and these can be material to more fully understand how light is the key to the psychic universe and psycho-kinesis.

6. EXERCISES FOR IMPROVING MIND CONTROL OVER MATTER

The only people who communicate with the spirit world are those who believe that it exists. The only people who talk to God are those who believe that He exists. The only people who receive answers from God are those who believe that He answers when we ask Him a question. The only people who believe that it's evil spirits or the devil answering when we ask God a question are those who believe that God will allow the devil to deceive us when we ask God a question.

Convince Yourself That You Can Control Matter

Children are easier to convince that God exists than adults.

Jesus said, "Except you become as little children you cannot see the Kingdom of God." *(Matt. 18:3)*

While still a child I became convinced that God existed, I could talk to Him and He would respond. I was convinced that His response would be primarily in action; He would move the world for me if I asked him to do this.

After being convinced that God was real, I agreed with Him to try to use His methods, as taught by Jesus, throughout my life.

I asked Him what my vocation in life should be, and He told me to build space ships—in 1939! No effort, except basic research, was in progress in space travel at that time, but I was convinced that God had told me to train for space-vehicle design work.

I began at that time, 11 years old, drawing space ships, and about 25 years later, I helped in the design of the *Saturn V* Moon Vehicle. At 43 years of age, I worked on the first NASA Skylab scheduled to be launched in 1973.

I had asked God to help me attain an education, which was a big request for the son of a tenant farmer!

He responded by presenting me with a four-year college scholarship which took me through to a BS in physics—but even more, because I was also presented the GI Bill after serving in the Navy for three years, I was able to obtain an MS in physics.

But why would a space ship designer take physics in college?

I had no idea what to take, and I certainly wasn't going to tell my college counselor in 1947 that I planned to design space ships.

Physics turned out to be the right course because it gave me what I needed in engineering, but more important, it gave me knowledge of the physical universe.

A few years before *Cosmic Mysteries* was published, my concept of a super-being was but a small view of the total God. Because of my change in the "God-concept," I felt the "universal intelligence" or "energy intelligence" were better terms; therefore, when I use the term God I mean much more than the religious God.

Because of my life's experiences I am convinced that God is answering my questions with actions and ideas. But am I convinced that I can mentally link with universal intelligence to move an object?

Late one night when I was in close contact with the psychic world, I had a strong desire to move an object with my mind. I asked for help to move a small plastic toy tile which was laying on the hearth. I concentrated hard on the tile, which was one-half inch square, trying to cause it to rise. It did! But not exactly like I had in mind. I heard a voice like my mind speaking to me, which said, "If you want that tile moved, get up and move it!" And I did. Thus the tile moved.

I gained much from this experience, because the message continued to inform me that in this physical universe, the natural way of P-K is for the psychic signal to come through to the physical brain in the form of a coded signal of light, thus giving the person the idea to move the object. The message did not rule out direct mind over matter, but there are natural laws which must be followed when the mind moves matter.

The stronger natural law which must be obeyed to practice mind over matter is to be convinced that you can move that mountain and it will be moved. If you are convinced that you can't move out of bed, then you can't; however, if you are convinced that you can make the bed rise through the air with you in it, you can, and the bed will rise as requested. Of this I am firmly convinced–the natural law of P-K is confidence.

The objects I have been convinced I should move, have moved, not in a way for me to become famous as a psychic person who commands the powers of the occult world, but in other ways that are more rewarding to me. The objects which have been most prominent are the moving of molecules in a person's body which will heal and keep him healthy.

Convince yourself that you can be healthy and you will be. Convince yourself that you can be healed and you will be. But it's easier for most of us to be convinced that God can heal us, which He can, so the same results are obtained. When we are convinced that God will move an object if we ask Him, we may think, "What useful purpose will this P-K accomplish?" Because we have included God in our activities, we are more likely to expend our powers in moving objects which need to be moved.

Another very important reason for depending upon a higher intelligence to move objects is because we need more than a human intelligence to safely practice P-K.

Meditation Exercises to Develop Better Reception

Meditation is a method which is often used by various religious and spiritualist groups to improve ESP or contact with the energy intelligence. In some cases, meditation is nothing more than a unique process for curing insomnia—it puts us to sleep. To meditate, we normally relax the body and mind, trying to think about a void. And usually when we think about nothing, we go to sleep. One meditation exercise which is beneficial to many people and still keeps them awake is as follows: 1. Sit in a comfortable chair and relax the body and mind. 2. Close the eyes and do not try to think about anything in particular. 3. Turn the thoughts inward and look for colors or pictures in the mind. These patterns are not produced because light filters through the eyelids to stimulate the retina of the eye, since I have closed my eyes in a cave without light and could still see colors and patterns. After the eyes have been closed for awhile, we shall begin to see colored patterns. These colored patterns will be random shapes, kaleidoscope fashion; now and then we shall see a picture, scene, or some event. 4. Follow these pictures as they show up in the mind. Possibly these pictures will then begin to develop a consistent story or pattern, which may be a prediction of some future event or just a repeat of something that has occurred to us in the last few days. Sometimes when we are watching these patterns, our mind will also begin to race. This can be primarily the subconscious part of the mind, which is beginning to function. We may call it imagination. Our imagination will begin to develop a dreamlike story without conscious effort. Many times when we have a common, daily problem which we are trying to resolve, we can use the meditation technique which causes many possible solutions to our problem to run through our mind, and one of these answers will be the correct or best one. As we meditate, we should be using the intelligence and knowledge of our minds with all of the capability within us. At the same time, we should continually ask the Holy Spirit to guide our subconscious mind and conscious mind in arriving at the correct answer. When we have exhausted all of our intellectual capabilities and feel that we have arrived at the best answer, we assume that this is the right answer to our question, while all the time remaining open-minded and considering possible changes as the Holy Spirit guides. If we err in judging the correct answer, the Holy Spirit will continue to speak through our subconscious, so that we cannot continue to proceed in the wrong direction. Meditation is a method of obtaining answers to questions, but most important of all, we should take action using psychic powers based upon the best answers.

Don't Consciously Judge Information

When a question has been asked, when information is sought, and an answer is desired from the universal intelligence, if there is the possibility of an answer to the question in literature,we should seek the answer there first. We should read and study; we should also talk to other individuals and consider their contributions. As we receive information which may be the answer we seek, but again may not, we should not consciously judge (accept or reject) material being received. *Matthew 7:1* reads, "Judge not, that ye be not judged." This verse normally is applied to the judging of people as to whether or not they are morally good or bad. However, this verse could also very aptly apply to the judging of information which is received by our brain. We should not judge the information we receive, such as various philosophies and religions of this world and many people's ideas of possible answers to our problems, but file the information in the brain. We can listen to the various comments of people, study the teachings of the Bible, and from these we may form some opinions, but it is better to be open minded. Simply ask God to formulate our thinking, without prejudice, through the working of the Holy Spirit, who can exert influence on the subconscious mind, thus forming beliefs without us realizing it, until someone asks us what we believe. Then we shall discover within our minds an established belief, placed there by God using our ESP ability!

The well-known clairvoyant, E. Lewis Russell,[1] expresses his opinion about judging as follows: "You must change your mental attitude so that no matter what anyone does or says, it will seem neither right nor wrong, but just something that is."

If we meditate to establish contact with God, then allow the Holy Spirit to formulate our beliefs, we can master great powers.

The primary result of an improved communication link is apparently psycho-kinesis, from an outward viewpoint, since the primary characteristics of many great psychics have been their ability to heal others, walk on water or air, change an object from one form to another, and move objects through the air. Less obvious powers gained by an improved communication link with

---

[1]Editors of *Fate Magazine, The Strange World of the Occult,* Paperback Library, Inc., New York, 1968, Clark Pub. Co., 1959.

the universal mind are control of self, a desire to use psychic powers to help those without such powers, and a desire not to advertise these powers.

Psychic Control by Suggestion

There are too many well-authenticated cases of psychokinesis for us to doubt that, at least in some instances, the mind can control matter. New evidence now seems to prove that the conscious mind in a way never before imagined, can also control our body functions and even control severe nerve sensations such as pain.

Sheila Ostrander and Lynn Schroeder[2] report on experiments with "suggestology" conducted in Bulgaria. Although there is some semblance to hypnosis, there is one major difference. In hypnosis, the hypnotist has control of the subject's mind; the subject is in a state of deep sleep or trance and he is not usually aware of what is going on around him. In suggestology the subject is in complete control of his mind and is aware at all times of what is occurring and what he is doing. The semblance is that just as there is a hypnotist in hypnosis, there is a leader in suggestology who helps the subject attain and keep the frame of mind necessary for him to make the ultimate use of his mind.

This technique was used in Bulgaria for many forms of healing, but probably the most dramatic experiments were in the use of mind control for anesthesia in surgery. The first major operation using mind control as the only form of anesthesia was performed in Byl ovo, Bulgaria, on August 24, 1965. The patient requested of Dr. Lozanov, the Bulgarian scientist who devised the techniques, that suggestology be used for anesthesia in the hernia operation which he was to undergo.

Minor surgery had previously been accomplished with the use of mind control as the only anesthesia, but never anything of this magnitude. This operation would require at least an hour to perform. The technique having been explained to them, Dr. Ivan Kalpov and Dr. Vasily Tanev agreed to perform the operation

---

[2]Ostrander, Sheila and Schroeder, Lynn, *Psychic Discoveries Behind the Iron Curtain*, Bantam Books, 1971; Prentice-Hall, Inc., Englewood Cliffs, New Jersey, 1970.

which would not only be televised, but also filmed for complete documentation.

Although he was fully awake during the entire procedure and clearly remembered each step of the operation, the patient at no time felt any pain. He was able to laugh and joke with the doctors as they cut a 2-inch incision in his abdomen, removed the hernia, and sutured the incision. He not only felt no pain, but through mind control of his blood flow, he was able to restrict the blood to the area of the operation so that there was little blood loss. His recuperation was rapid. Having given his body a suggestion to that effect, the incision healed more rapidly than normal.

Experiments have shown that an atmosphere of calm and peacefulness is of utmost importance to the success of this technique. It is necessary that the patient be able to attain a feeling of deep relaxation while at the same time remaining fully awake and in complete control of his mind and mental faculties. This is apparently the same state of mind that is most conducive to success in any exercise of ESP abilities or other psychic powers.

Major benefits can be obtained from mastery of this form of psycho-kinesis, not only from use in surgery, both major and minor, but to help us meet the strains of everyday life.

Scientific Research Produces Convincing Evidence

In Durham, North Carolina, a research team is trying to find scientific evidence of something a carpenter from Bethlehem said nearly 2,000 years ago—that there is life after death. The results of their research have uncovered several evidences of psycho-kinesis. The research team has investigated many mysterious happenings which are typical of those recorded throughout history.

So far, they have neither proved nor disproved that a human being's soul or any other part of him lives after his body dies, but they are convinced that such phenomena as extrasensory perception and objects flying through the air for no apparent reason do exist.

The organization, called the Psychical Research Foundation, was founded in 1961. Its headquarters is in two yellow frame houses in a residential neighborhood of Durham.

The director, W.G. Roll, a graduate of Oxford University, and others connected with the foundation say a part of the reason for their slow progress is that many scientists think their studies are a waste of time.

Consequently, little of the big chunks of money used to finance scientific research finds its way to the foundation. The bulk of the foundation's financing comes from bequests.

Some of the work of the foundation has been the investigation of poltergeists, the unexplained movement of objects. The researchers say they have witnessed such occurrences.

Persons connected with the foundation are reluctant to talk about such studies, for two reasons: a fear that reporters will see the work as unscientific ghost-chasing, and because they are afraid information on specific families may lead to crank telephone calls and other pranks.

Olive Hill Poltergeist

A form of psycho-kinesis which may be controlled by exercising this technique is the case of poltergeist occurrences. This psycho-kinesis is usually destructive, is random moving and breaks objects, and is often associated with a mentally disturbed young person.

In Olive Hill, Kentucky, in 1969, a poltergeist caused destruction through five houses and left family members emotionally distraught.

At first, neighbors were dubious of events reported in the John Callihan home on Henderson Branch, for only a few persons, principally family members, could swear they had seen mysterious movements and the cracking of glass by invisible hands. It was real enough for the Callihans, though, and they moved to Zimmerman Hill, a half-mile away. The move brought two weeks of peace, after which, conditions were worse than before.

A pair of psychical researchers from Durham, North Carolina associated with Duke University, came and watched for several days. Before leaving they verified the occurrences and said they were due to psycho-kinesis.

The preternatural events seemed to center around a 12-year-old grandson of the family. His mother, a member of Jehovah's Witnesses, follows that church's teachings that such unexplained happenings are the work of demons. It was because of this belief that the two researchers returned to Durham. They did advise a program of help based on personal study by a psychiatrist and physician.

The occurrences began on Nov. 15, 1968, in the Henderson Branch house, where the elder Callihans had lived about two years. And it was on Dec. 7 that the weird movements first began in the new home.

The weekend following the visit of the two researchers was marked by two more nights of violent movement. The researchers and others agreed that the movements coincided with the activity and emotions of the grandson.

After the boy's parents isolated him in their home, movements started there and followed him into the homes of two uncles.

The first occurrence in Henderson Branch was a shocker. With only a few of the family about, glass in mirrors and picture frames began to snap. The first bad night in the second house included a manifestation of a pale, thin man. Mrs. Callihan and Archie, who said they saw the apparition, were sure it resembled her brother who died 13 years ago.

At first doubtful of what he had heard, the movements in the house convinced the father that something was going on. He considered it to be a curse.

The two researchers, W.G. Roll and John Stump, of the Institute for Psychical Research, left this opinion on the happenings, which they termed typical poltergeist phenomena.

"We have come up against this kind of process in other investigations of this type, which we refer to as psycho-kinesis, or P-K—a mind-over-matter effect.

"This term refers to an energy that, in all likelihood, everybody possesses. It is similar to other human faculties, but with most of us it operates on a confined scale and is not noticeable.

"It is a natural and normal faculty or force which, however, is not under the conscious control of anyone. No one wants, or wills, these things to happen."

Roll says most poltergeist cases involve a so-called "agent," someone whose presence seems to be connected with the movement of the objects.

That was the case, said Roll, in Miami where objects reportedly had been flying off of shelves in a warehouse in which novelty items were stored. The breakings were always found to occur in the presence of an anxiety-plagued young Cuban who worked in the warehouse.

Roll checked the warehouse for fraud and found no wires or other devices that could cause the objects to fly through the air. He said he placed several specific objects on shelves in positions where it would be impossible for them simply to fall.

Roll said he examined the objects in advance and they were normal, but even these flew through the air. He saw one of the objects dashed to pieces far from where it had been positioned.

No one was in the warehouse area who could have hurled the objects to the floor, Roll said. The breakings remain a mystery.

In Jacksonville, Florida, for instance, two investigators from the foundation visited a house where an apparition reportedly had been seen several times.

One investigator, Dr. John Artley, an electrical engineering professor at Duke University, said he saw a glowing light "about the size of a football" at the foot of a bed, where seconds before he had seen nothing. Then it disappeared.

Although the Durham research team has neither proven nor disproven that there is life after death, they have very firm evidence that unknown forces are at work moving objects and producing lights, which means that these unexplained events can be caused by forces in the psychic universe, thus adding to our evidences that a link-up with the psychic universe can give us powers to move objects with our mind.

As the evidences of the psychic universe continue to increase, more and more people in professional occupations are observing and investigating unusual occult phenomena, including many cases of objects moving by unknown, mysterious forces.

Possible Subconscious P-K

Robert A. Bradley,[3] a medical doctor, has observed several cases of P-K, one of which occurred one day when he reached for a heavily weighted cigar lighter which was sitting on a table. He

---

[3]Bradley, Robert A. and Bradley, D., *Psychic Phenomena: Revelations and Experiences,* Parker Publishing Company, Inc., West Nyack, N.Y. 1967.

lived for many years in an old house which many times showed evidence of psychic occurrences. As his hand neared the lighter, he was amazed to see the lighter mysteriously rise above the table and move about a foot from his rigidly outstretched hand. Then he saw the possessed, inanimate object silently come to rest on its side on the table.

After he recovered from his initial shock of seeing the lighter move under its own power, he examined it very closely but could find nothing abnormal about it. When he deliberately pushed it over it fell with a noisy metallic clink, not silently as it did after it floated away from him. He had no explanation for the floating lighter, but let us raise some questions.

Why did the lighter move when Dr. Bradley's hand approached it the first time and not the second time? Could Dr. Bradley have influenced the P-K of the lighter the first time without conscious thought but influenced the lighter the second time with conscious thought?

Dr. Bradley has a deep interest in the psychic; therefore, he may have linked with the psychic universe, causing the lighter to move under subconscious control of his mind, but when he began exercising normal mental control, the lighter moved at the push from his finger.

With faith as of a child, feats of P-K and other spiritual miracles may be even more possible. As a child psychic matters are more common, but adults usually try to convince the child that psychic experiences are all imagination. This naturally causes normal children to reject spiritual experiences until they no longer have psychic experiences at all or ignore those which they experience.

Dr. Bradley observed several other P-K phenomena while living in his old "haunted" house. One of these was observed when he returned from a shopping trip. He found the reception hall in a shambles. He reported that plants were uprooted, dirt was scattered about, and decorative furnishings were toppled over. Again, he could find no satisfactory explanation for the chaos, except that some powerful forces from the occult must have been active.

Many other times the psychic forces were evident, as lamps would click on for no apparent reason. Not just one lamp at a time, but two lamps would come on simultaneously. Since both lamps were on the same circuit as a TV set which was already on, when the lamps mysteriously came on, they did not come on from a common switch being turned on. When examined closely, one lamp switch was on the second position of the three-way switch and the other was on the third position. Those persons present with Dr. Bradley when the lights came on heard no clicks, but manual operation produced clearly audible clicks.

At another time while electrical work was being performed on Dr. Bradley's haunted house, a yellow light came on, which did not at once seem supernormal since an electrician was working on the wiring, but further investigation showed the electrician to be in a supply room and not tampering with the electrical circuits.

In a period of about one month, the Bradleys experienced the strange case of one of two bedroom lamps going on spontaneously three different times, and one went off mysteriously once. One evening when a lamp lit up, a popping noise was heard on the ceiling. Then other lights came on or went off for no apparent reason except psychical forces during this siege of psycho-kinetic operating lights.

One night a bedroom light began acting up, with the switch clicking on and off but the lamp not lighting up. Then the lamp began going on and off as the switch continued to click for a total of 12 times, according to Dr. Bradley.

Another direct evidence of P-K was the bobbing around of a large brass chandelier which was suspended by a chain from the ceiling. This strange sight was suspected to be caused by an earth tremor at first, but no other chandeliers were moving and the Bradleys felt no movement of the house.

These are but a few of the many psychic experiences told by Dr. Bradley, who seemed to have encountered many more unexplainable events than most people. Could these experiences have been caused by Dr. Bradley because he was subconsciously willing them to occur? Or is it possible that the mind can function in the psychic realm in a manner similar to the way the mind controls involuntary body functions, such as blood pressure, body temperature, heart beat rate, etc.?

Medical science is studying how the mind subconsciously controls the body functions, and as science gains knowledge, we have greater confidence in our ability to be masters of our physical bodies. Why shouldn't we also gain confidence in our ability to control psychic phenonema as we observe these psychic events?

All events affecting the senses should be used to increase knowledge, confidence, and understanding of the psychic and physical worlds. Some peculiar, yet normal events can stimulate thinking so that an answer to a question can be obtained through use of the intelligence and the imagination. One such event occurred on September 14, 1968.

The Case of the Disappearing Wire

Early on this beautiful Saturday morning, I was outside enjoying the cool, clear, fresh morning air. As I looked around at the clear sky, except for a few small clouds, I remembered UFO stories told the night before by Red Harper, a Baptist Evangelist. The stories had been very convincing, and I wondered if vehicles from outside the earth were near at that time. I decided to request that one appear so I could be finally and completely convinced that UFO's as space visitors, actually exist. I called on energy intelligence to bring in a UFO, really feeling that he could do this as a visual evidence that there were powerful, higher intelligent beings near and available for communication. I requested, and looked, but the sky remained clear of unusual objects. After a few minutes' waiting and looking, I discontinued the experiment.

About two hours later, I was working on an electric cattle fence. I laid a piece of shiny, number 16 wire, which was doubled and bent into an irregular shape and about 3 feet long, on the ground in grass and weeds beside a metal post that I was trying to pull out of the ground. I also laid a hammer down close to the wire. After pulling the post out of the ground, I moved it about 5 feet and drove it back into the ground using the hammer. I then went over to pick up the wire, but it wasn't where I had dropped it. I searched diligently for the wire all around the area for about ten minutes before I gave up and left. All the time I was looking, I was thinking about my earlier request for a UFO to appear, wondering if there was a message in my lack of success in locating the wire.

I commented to my wife and children about the apparent mysterious disappearance of the wire, but realized it was probably no more mysterious than some mental block which prevented me from seeing the wire which was probably where I had dropped it.

The next afternoon I went back to the same spot and walked directly, unhesitatingly to the wire and picked it up! It was lying in a ragweed about 2 feet off the ground, 5 feet from where I thought I had placed it.

Could such occurrences be a method of higher intelligence contacting us? Whether the wire had been actually moved, made invisible, taken away, or whether I had been psychologically affected so that I could not see the wire, I had serious thoughts about methods used by a higher intelligence to contact us. I received a message which added to my confidence in psychic powers by analyzing what had happened. It may have been the correct interpretation—a higher intelligence contacting us may use communication methods which require use of our senses, plus reasoning.

Psychic occurrences are often associated with people who are expecting them, which indicates that people trigger P-K feats.

The subconscious mind which controls many body functions without conscious effort, could also control psycho-kinesis and other psychic phenomena. The subconscious mind of a skilled athlete is trained to control the body muscles more accurately than the conscious mind can control them.

As an example, a bowler will try to control his body, steps, arm, and hand the same way each time he aims for a strike. Sometimes he will have a strike, while other times he will leave some pins standing, even though he will consciously try to deliver the ball in exactly the same way each time. The bowler is consciously trying to learn how to obtain a strike each time, but his conscious mind does not know how.

The subconscious mind will have to develop confidence that it can control the body before the bowler becomes proficient in delivering the ball. The mind will learn how to move each body muscle in minute detail to control the ball so that it will roll to the exact spot required to obtain a strike on ten pins. If the subconscious mind can learn to do what the conscious mind cannot, in control of body functions, possibly the subconscious mind can be trained to control P-K by moving objects not physically connected to the brain the way muscles are connected.

Learn and Practice the Rules of the Game

There may be several parallels between learning how to control a bowling ball and learning how to control P-K. There may be rules of the P-K game that must be followed to obtain skill in P-K.

To establish a set of rules for a game which is as nebulous as P-K or other psychic phenomena may seem impossible, but there may be a way to arrive at the rules.

All of the rules seem to be patterned after those taught by the world's most powerful psychic, Jesus Christ. These rules are summarized in the well-known Golden Rule, "Do unto others as you would have them do unto you."

If a person does not follow this rule, possibly he can still have psychic powers, but this does not seem to fit the case histories of the world's great psychics, who seemed to have a deep concern for their fellowman.

One of the less well-known psychics who seems to be following the rule of helping others is Kathryn Kuhlman,[4] who seems to have psychic powers to heal, and demonstrates P-K powers which cause people to fall over when she touches them. In a healing service, she is reported to leave literally scores of people lying in the aisles. As she touched a person to heal him, he would keel over on the floor, as if knocked out by her touch. She put her hand on the lower jaw just beneath the ear of a woman and she fell to the floor. However, when the woman was helped up off the floor and asked how she felt, she said, "Wonderful. It was a sort of electricity. I was just illuminated."

For some strange reason, all who fell were adults who had followed close behind Kuhlman. As she touched one small boy, he just stood grinning while she moved on to the next person.

Two Catholic priests, standing on the stage where Miss Kuhlman had preached, fell over when she touched them. One of them, the Rev. John Lane, a Jesuit, is an associate Pastor at Holy Family Church in Chicago.

Mrs. Eleanor Werch, 52, of Oshkosh, Wisconsin, said she walked without crutches for the first time in ten years.

Sister Ethel Denn, a Catholic nun from Mankato, Minnesota, said she was relieved of pains and swelling in her legs suffered over the last ten years.

Another nun, Sister Honora, from Holy Trinity Convent,

---

[4]Bowman, James H., "Faith-Healer's Touch Seems to Cure Many Ills." *Chicago Daily News* Service, Oct. 23, 1971.

Westmont, Illinois, a member of the sisters of Christian Charity for 67 years, said she was cured of arthritis.

Mrs. Astrid Kolnes, a native of Norway, said she no longer felt a sharp abdominal pain from cancer.

Mrs. Kolnes came up from the overflow crowd one floor below, as did many others. These had heard Miss Kuhlman on a public-address system but had not seen her.

"I felt my heart pounding," she said, describing the sensation of being cured. "Something warm came over me."

Marie Donofrio, Oak Park, Illinois, a member of St. Angela Roman Catholic Church, said she had suffered from glaucoma for 15 years. Without glasses, she counted the fingers on Miss Kuhlman's hands as Miss Kuhlman held them up.

Scores of men and women came to the stage saying they were healed. Several left wheelchairs. Some threw away crutches or canes. All received the touch at the cheekbone that in most cases knocked them over.

Kathryn Kuhlman used her psychic power, which could knock people down, to heal physical problems. She practiced the rules for the use of her psychic powers, as she understood them, with fantastic results.

As we obtain control of greater psychic forces, we should also practice the correct rules so that others may benefit from our special gift.

Where one person will have a special psychic talent to heal, another will have the ability to move objects with his mind, and another will develop ability to obtain ideas and information from the unobstructed universe.

Several cases of having ideas and asking for confirmation have been related already. Another case of apparent communication with the universal mind was when I asked God the relationship between gravity and psychic forces. The ideas which I received in response to my query seemed to be a special case of psychic force moving the brain cells so that the ideas were constructed in my mind.

The basic question which I asked was, "What is gravity?"

As I waited for an answer, I doodled on the corner of a sheet of paper without being aware of what I was drawing. I drew three circles representing an atom containing a nucleus and two electrons. But, then I drew two "v's" over each of the electrons which seemed to press the electrons toward the nucleus.

After the drawing was complete, I became aware of it and wondered if it contained an answer about gravity. I understood the symbols to mean that the v's represented the basic psychic forces which "press" matter together in the physical universe.

Gravity is not a pulling force between physical bodies but it is a result of the psychic force pushing the physical universe together. Gravity is always a natural characteristic of a physical body, because all physical objects displace a minute amount of psychic material of the unobstructed universe which creates an imbalance around the object, thus the psychic material trying to return to the volume which the object occupies produces a psychic force on the object.

When we stand on the earth's surface, we say gravity holds us with a force of one "g"; however, it may be possible that this nebulous psychic force is pressing down upon us with a force of one g. The reason that the same force is not pushing on the bottoms of our feet is because the earth is in the way or interferes with the force.

The more massive the object, the greater the shielding effect for psychic forces, thus a greater push or higher g's.

If we can redirect the psychic forces, we can cause objects to rise or move. We can lift ourselves by cutting off psychic forces pressing us to the earth and allowing psychic forces against the bottom of our feet to lift us. However, we can also move objects by releasing photons in a controlled manner so that the object is pushed by the departing photons.

From a scientific viewpoint, I have little supporting evidence to call the above ideas about gravity a theory, because the ideas are not based upon experiments or observation but only upon the possibility that the ideas could have been given to me by a higher intelligence who understands much more about gravity than we understand.

He Conquered with P-K

The famous psychic, Doc Anderson,[5] of Rossville, Georgia, used a very simple technique to control psycho-kinetic forces which gained fame and success for him. He recognized, while a

---

[5]Smith, Robert E., *The Man Who Sees Tomorrow,* Paperback Library, New York, N.Y., 1970.

boxer for a circus, that he could use his mind to win a bout. By thinking what he wanted to happen, it would. When he wanted to win, he thought hard about the particular results he desired, either more power for his muscles or more resistance to his opponent's muscles. He was so successful at using psycho-kinesis while boxing that he won too many fights and could not find challengers; therefore, he would turn off his psycho-kinetic ability to give his opponents a chance to win.

He also used psycho-kinesis to lift tremendous weights, which gained him the title of the world's weight lifting champ. He would lift several men, a car, hundreds of pounds of dumbbells, and perform many other superhuman feats by thinking that psychic forces helped him.

As his utilization of the supernatural increased, so did his fame. Then he settled in Rossville, Georgia where thousands of people visit him yearly for advice about the future and how to solve daily problems. There at Doc's office, Jerry Johnson, a NASA engineer and friend of the writer, visited Doc Anderson, who had an office full of people waiting to see him.

Jerry talked to Doc about the extent of his psychic powers and his technique for tapping these mysterious forces. Doc told Jerry that concentration was his key. He would think very hard about what he wanted to happen and it would. He had demonstrated his keen psycho-kinetic ability by shattering a glass with his mind! In this unprecedented test of a human mind controlling psycho-kinetic forces, he mentally visualized the glass broken so realistically, that the glass actually broke. Doc gave Jerry a copy of a picture taken of Doc and three witnesses at the instant the glass shattered to bits as Doc's powerful mind channeled the universal force to the glass.

If Doc Anderson can tap the psychic forces, so can anyone who follows the technique of developing confidence and concentration. And although he has gained fame and wealth, he uses his powers with discretion, primarily in trying to help others tap his source of power. He would take no money from Jerry Johnson, even though he had spent about one hour talking to Jerry, because he did not feel that Jerry needed his special abilities. Jerry was interested in learning how natural psychic forces can be utilized by the normal person.

Jerry Johnson, like the writer, is a scientist who has been convinced by people like Doc Anderson and his own psychic experiences that psycho-kinesis is available for our use if we are willing to utilize it.

He Stares at a Glass of Water to Obtain Psychic Control

Olof Jonsson[6] is a Chicago engineer and one of the most rigidly tested psychics of our time.

A native of Sweden and well-known there for his powers in levitating objects, predicting the future, solving mysteries clairvoyantly, and performing unbelievable tricks with decks of cards which he never touches, Jonsson came to this country for the purpose of having his psychic ability tested scientifically. Many tests have been made both in this country and in Sweden, so that the credibility of Jonsson's feats have been well established.

His personal beliefs include a purposeful universe with a Divine Plan that will in the end be harmonious. He believes that the best technique for reaching this complete satisfaction that comes from a oneness with God is through personal meditation.

Believing that every person has psychic ability if he will only develop it, he does not recommend the use of a Ouija Board. Rather, he recommends filling a glass with water and setting it on the table before you. Stare at the water and erase all thoughts from your mind. Think of nothing, but just concentrate on the water. When you feel that the proper conditioning has been met, then you can practice such things as guessing cards from an ESP deck or moving objects with your mind.

Once you have achieved the ability to let your subconscious mind rise above the conscious, the glass of water is no longer necessary. It is merely a physical object on which to focus your attention. With more and more practice, it becomes easier to achieve the altered state of consciousness necessary for the exercise of your psychic abilities.

Jonsson is of the opinion that a person may derive many

---

[6]Steiger, Brad, and Jonsson, Olof *The Psychic Feats of Olof Jonsson,* Prentice-Hall, Inc., Englewood Cliffs, N.J., 1971.

important benefits from this heightened psychic ability. One that he feels is of the utmost importance is, "a great calm and peace that suffuses one's soul and makes him harmonious with the universe. This sense of harmony places the minor distractions of our earthly life in their proper perspective and enables the sensitive to be serene and tranquil wherever they may be."

Final Evidence That Psychic Requests Are Answered

As if much of this chapter was being handed to me by the universal mind, this final, extremely unusual, true story was given to me at this time, just as I was concluding this chapter. It is an uncanny feeling to have a complete stranger start telling me a strange but factual story which seemed to be exactly the evidence I was seeking that psychic forces produce light in the physical universe.

Light being produced in the physical world from signals in the psychic world was confirmed in my mind by a very unusual response I received from a request to the universal mind for a confirmation of this idea. Light, I felt, is the link, and possibly the only link, between this universe and the psychic universe. Light is required when a psychic receives a message. Light is required when a person is "faith-healed." And light is seen when a dead person appears in an image of his physical body.

I sensed that the "window light" seen by Laura and Allen Hayes was a message to me, that light is a window into the psychic universe. I suspected even more strongly that light is the link, a few days after the window light incident, when friends dropped in to see us and brought a house guest of theirs who related a very unusual story of a young girl who returned from the dead.

How Adrian Carlton Used Light to Return to the Physical World

This story was related to me on Dec. 5, 1971, just one month after the "window light" was seen by Laura and Allen. The impression I received was that Jamie Green, who told me the story, had been guided to me all the way from California to

Alabama which seemed to be additional confirmation that spirits can produce light.

This is the story as Jamie related it. In the summer of 1971 a 17-year-old art student of his was shot and killed, which is a shocking end to some stories, but in this case she was seen many times by various people, including Jamie, after her death. Adrian Carlton, the girl who was shot, was seen four times by Jamie; she was seen by Gail, a close friend; her parents; and several members of an I AM type group in Santa Barbara, California where Adrian had lived and died. She was seen mostly by Gail, in whose room Jamie saw her twice.

Jamie had gone to visit Gail, walked into her room, and saw Adrian sitting in a high-back rocker. Gail was not home. Jamie awkwardly spoke to Adrian by name, but she did not respond. With a very eerie feeling, he turned and walked out of the room. He thought he saw her again, hitch-hiking, and stopped to pick her up. He had passed her before he could stop. When he backed up to where she had been standing, being certain of who she was, she was no longer there. He told other members of this psychic group that he had seen her, and some of them also reported seeing her at another location on the street hitch-hiking the same night.

The group decided to locate her and ask why she was appearing. They located her at Gail's apartment and began communicating with her by psychic mind reading.

Jamie was with the group, saw Adrian, but could not communicate with her. He said that Adrian told the others she did not want to leave her friends.

The group tried to convince her that it was best for her to discontinue appearing in this world, since she frightened many people, and that she would be happier with those in her same spiritual condition. The group discussion with her apparently helped, because she did not appear after that.

Jamie is an art instructor at the University of California in Santa Barbara, who has never had such an experience before. He is firmly convinced that Adrian was able to materialize a body of light which he and many others saw. He said her body was transparent but distinct enough to look like an actual person.

I wondered if there was some special significance to her

name, the same as my first name and the same last initial. I felt that this was also a special confirmation, but there was yet another confirmation that light is the link to psychic powers.

This other confirmation was that Jamie told me about a friend who had just earned her college degree. She was now working with the Santa Barbara group in the investigation of the phenomenon of light associated with psychic occurrences. I had been looking for a person with her educational background and interest to discuss my theories.

Once again, a man who had traveled 2,000 miles gave the contact I sought, as if psychic forces brought him to me in response to my request for confirmation of the ideas about light being a window into the spirit universe.

As I have attempted to present ways of exercising the mind to control psychic force, the universal mind seemed to be giving me story after story and many ideas, which confirmed my theory that psychic abilities are available if we just convince ourselves that P-K and other psychic abilities are possible—after we establish a communication link with the universal mind. Since so many scientific facts and true stories are available to convince us, we can move on in psychic development by observing the rules of the game, primarily using powers to help others. Whereas I develop psychic ability to receive information about the natural and psychic universe, others may receive powers in P-K, telling the future, faith-healing, or other areas.

Regardless of the particular psychic abilities we develop, we shall all receive tremendous rewards for our efforts, primary of which will be a sense of satisfaction, happiness, and a feeling that we are successful. We shall realize that this life has been spent in developing ourselves for a greater future.

As has been requested before, if the reader will report his experiences, these will give confidence to many others to try communicating with the universal mind. With more people using psychic powers, the earth will become a better environment for full awareness of universal intelligence.

As a word of caution, when we hear unusual stories, such as the one told by Jamie Green, we should not accept the story as fact without sound justification. I checked Green's story with other people whom he involved and found that some basic parts of his story could be verified while other parts were in conflict with what others knew about the events.

Those who knew Green considered him to have a good imagination. Those checked agreed to the name of the girl who was murdered, but no one would admit having seen her ghost. One person said she felt Adrian's vibrations and the group performed a ceremony of freeing her spirit from the physical world.

With the items which could be substantiated, there was a definite message from the spirit world about the link of light between the spirit and physical universes.

7. STRANGE POWERS OF THE MIND

The human mind is a mystery. The more we attempt to learn about the functioning of the mind, the more mysterious it becomes. A major obstacle in resolving this mystery is that we have only our finite minds for solving the mystery; therefore, we have a mystery trying to resolve the mystery. How does the mind function? What is extrasensory perception and how does it work? What's the limit of memory capacity in a brain? What is the limit of intelligence of a brain? How do human brains unite to accomplish great feats, such as landing men on the moon, developing the atomic bomb, and inventing TV, radar, automobiles, and airplanes? How does the imagination work? How can so many ideas be formulated in the psychological realm? Why are there so many types of religions, beliefs, theories, guesses? Are there no limits to the strange powers of the mind?

An Extra-Terrestrial Man Demonstrates Fantastic Mental Powers

The most famous and well-known individual who demonstrated more unusual powers than any other man who has ever lived on the earth is Jesus Christ of Nazareth. The powers which he exercised are so unusual, so miraculous, that many people believe he performed miracles because he followed, not natural laws, but some system especially reserved for God. Others do not believe he did anything by the power of the mind, because they consider these stories of miracles too fantastic to be true. He began his unusual demonstration of mental ability by first changing water into wine at the feast in Cana of Galilee.

> Jesus saith unto them, Fill the waterpots with water. And they filled them up to the brim. And he saith unto them, Draw out now, and bear into the governor of the feast. And they bore it. When the ruler of the feast had tasted the water that was made wine, and knew not whence it was (but the servants knew), the governor of the feast called the bridegroom. And saith unto him, Every man at the beginning doth set forth good wine; and when men have well drunk, then that which is worse; but thou hast kept the good wine until now. This beginning of miracles did Jesus in Cana of Galilee, and manifested forth his glory; and his disciples believed in him. *John 2:7-11*

He had the power to heal.

> When Jesus saw him lie, and knew that he had been now a long time in that case, he saith unto him, Wilt thou be made whole? The impotent man answered him, Sir, I have no man, when the water is troubled, to put me into the pool: but while I am coming, another steppeth down before me. Jesus saith unto him, Rise, take up thy bed, and walk. And immediately the man was made whole, and took up his bed, and walked: and on the same day was the sabbath. *John 5:6-9*

He had the power to multiply five loaves and two fishes into sufficient food to feed over 5,000 people.

> And Jesus said, Make the men sit down. Now there was much grass in the place. So the men sat down, in number about five thousand. And Jesus took the loaves; and when he had given thanks, he distributed to the disciples, and the disciples to them that were set down; and likewise of the fishes as much as they would. When they were filled, he said unto his disciples, Gather up the fragments that remain, that nothing be lost. Therefore they gathered them together, and filled twelve baskets with the fragments of the five barley loaves, which remained over and above unto them that had eaten. *John 6:10-13*

He also made the blind to see.

> And as Jesus passed by, he saw a man which was blind from his birth. . . . And said unto him, Go, wash in the pool of Siloam, (which is by interpretation Sent). He went his way therefore, and washed, and came seeing. *John 9:1, 7*

Probably one of his greatest miraculous feats was exercising the powers of his mind to raise Lazarus from the dead!

> And when he thus had spoken, he cried with a loud voice, Lazarus, come forth. And he that was dead came forth, bound hand and foot with graveclothes: and his face was bound about with a napkin. Jesus saith unto them, Loose him, and let him go. *John 11:43-44*

An even greater power of his mind was that he did not remain dead when crucified. He was placed in a tomb, but on the third day was seen alive again.

> But Mary stood without at the sepulchre weeping: and as she wept, she stooped down, and looked into the sepulchre. And seeth two angels in white sitting, the one at the head, and the other at the feet, where the body of Jesus had lain. And they say unto her, Woman, why weepest thou? She saith unto them, Because they have taken away my Lord, and I know not where they have laid him. And when she had thus said, she turned herself back, and saw Jesus standing, and knew not that it was Jesus. Jesus saith unto her, Woman, why weepest thou? She, supposing him to be the gardener, saith unto him, Sir, if thou have borne him hence, tell me where thou hast laid him, and I will take him away. *John 20:11-15*

He could also pass through the walls of a room.

> Then the same day at evening, being the first day of the week, when the doors were shut where the disciples were assembled for fear of the Jews, came Jesus and stood in the midst, and saith unto them, Peace be unto you. *John 20:19*

Yet, possibly the greatest power of all was his ability to control his great power. His powers were never used for his own gain or interest. What human on earth today, if he had powers like Christ, would not use them for his own gain? Could anyone have sufficient control of himself to withhold use of unlimited mental powers to prevent himself from being killed? Yet, Jesus did this. He allowed himself to be hung from a cross and crucified. Only a mind with powers far beyond anything we can visualize could exercise such stupendous control.

Mental Powers Available

After Christ arose into the universal transport cloud *(Acts 1:9)* and returned to heaven, many of his powers were bestowed upon his followers. The early believers, as reported in *Acts of the Apostles,* had unusual powers of healing. They could be understood in foreign languages. They could escape from a locked jail. And they could do other miraculous things. Since the time of the early Apostles and on up to the present, people have had, at random, unusual powers. Many of these powers did not develop through training, but are generally inherited abilities from birth or are acquired unintentionally sometime in life.

One of the strange and unusual qualities of a modern mind has been demonstrated by Ted Serios.[1] He has an amazing ability to impress images on photographic film.

A feat of this nature seems so unreasonable, so illogical, and unassociated with any of the known facts of science, that many scientific-minded people would discard Eisenbud's story as another wild science fiction tale. However, once an assumption is made that information is false, nothing more can be learned from the information even though it may be true. Since I developed a theory which would explain this phenomenon before hearing the story, and although I could accept the story as a point for consideration, I was surprised that there was a person with the capability that Serios exercised. The theory of how he impressed images on photographic film was presented in Chapter 1. This unusual ability indicates that Serios has a communication link with universal intelligence, who impresses the image on the film through P-K control.

Thoughts Can Move a Mountain

Jesus said in *Matthew 17:20* "... If ye have faith as a grain of mustard seed, ye shall say unto this mountain, Remove hence

---

[1]Eisenbud, Jule, *The World of Ted Serios,* William Morrow and Co., Inc., 1967.

to yonder place; and it shall remove; and nothing shall be impossible unto you." Does this mean literally that by thought we can move a mountain? Mountains have been moved by thought, when super-highways are built across our land. Many mountains or major portions of mountains are moved by bulldozers, and other heavy earth-moving equipment. Someone had the thoughts of cutting away the mountains before they were moved. Does this mean that by thinking about it and planning and spending the necessary money, furnishing the bulldozers and the drivers, that finally a mountain can be moved? It does require faith to do all of this.

The night when I attempted to use P-K to move the small piece of toy tile, I was conducting an experiment to determine if faith was available to move a small object. Since it requires only the faith of a grain of mustard seed to move a whole mountain, it seems that only a small amount of faith would be necessary to move a small object. However, faith the size of a grain of mustard seed may be a tremendous amount of faith, because faith is an idea, a mental quality. How much thinking does it require to be equivalent to a grain of mustard seed? Is all of the knowledge in our head more than a grain of mustard seed? Are all our beliefs combined equivalent to a physical seed? It is difficult to equate the non-physical to the physical. Faith is non-physical, the mustard seed is physical.

When the attempt was made to move the tile, it moved because I responded to a very distinct impression of a voice in my mind which said, "All right, if you want to move the object, get up, go over, and move it!" And I did, and the object was moved by an apparent signal coming to me and telling me to move the object.

Additional ideas also cascaded in my mind, such as: yes, objects can be moved by thinking alone, but that isn't the method for us to be using yet. Many controls and restrictions may be involved in moving objects by thought like rules for driving an automobile.

One of those who is reported to have moved objects by thought was a girl who lived in a rural area. She was the daughter of a Baptist deacon and discovered early in her life that she could move objects about her room. Through trial and error, she developed more control of the movement of objects until she could prevent a person from touching her if she so desired. After her unusual ability became known, she was in demand as a performer.

A typical performance would be to invite any man in the audience to come up and try to touch her. As the man approached her, he would be thrown back across the stage with tremendous force. It was claimed by skeptics that she was using a trick of some sort. No one determined exactly what her trick was.

In another demonstration, she would effortlessly lift a very heavy man sitting in a chair. With the man seated in the chair, she would place her hand under it and raise the entire chair and man completely over her head. She was tested while performing this demonstration by a group of scientists in Washington, D.C.

The scientists checked her weight, the man's weight, and the chair's weight, separately, and in combination during the performance. They found that when she was standing on the scales lifting the man in the chair, the measured weight was not as great as the separate weights of the three.

Anne Gehman[2] discovered, when she was quite young, that she had the unusual ability to cause a table to levitate. In 1968, she put on a demonstration for Jean Yothers in Cassadega, Florida. In this demonstration Anne used a small inconspicuous mahogany table, on top of which both she and Yothers, a writer for the *Orlando Sentinel,* placed their hands. The unorthodox procedure was to ask the table a question. According to Gehman, the table would be moved by spirits to answer "no" with two rocks of the table and "yes" with three. Apparently Anne persuaded the spirits not only to move the table two or three times, but also to move it back and forth, with the table gaining momentum until it was spinning madly around and around like a top. Mysteriously, it gradually lifted off the floor, then settled back. A theory which could explain the movement of the table is given in Chapter 8.

Poltergeists

A poltergeist is a spirit or ghost who throws objects around, often breaking and damaging them. In many cases, either a young

[2] *Orlando Sentinel,* April 21, 1968.

boy or girl has been associated with this unusual phenomenon.

Eileen Garrett[3] has investigated strange poltergeist occurrences. Eileen thought that poltergeists were usually associated with tragic experiences preceding a person's death. She postulated that the ghost of that unfortunate person remained in the vicinity of the tragedy, trying to attract the attention of someone by throwing objects about. She relates a strange poltergeist case.

The son of a retired admiral in the British Navy seemed to be associated with objects being thrown about in his father's home. The boy's mother had often heard unusual footsteps and noticed a disarrangement of shoes after they had moved into this eventful house. One day the admiral was seated at a table when the scotch and soda on the table began to mysteriously move away from him without any reason. As the surprised admiral gazed in open-mouthed astonishment, the glass slid all the way to the edge of the table, crashed to the floor, and shattered into many pieces. According to Garrett, the reason for an unhappy spirit being involved in this episode was because a relative had died and left a will which had been misplaced, and the spirit was trying to attract the attention of these people so they could locate the will. Through Eileen's help, the will was located and the poltergeist retired from the scene. Many other supernormal poltergeist cases have been reported in occult literature.

A Very Wise Stick

Henry Gross,[4] a water dowser, had an unusual stick, although it was actually a common forked stick which had been cut from a peach or apple tree. This stick had the astounding ability to answer profound questions about water. Henry Gross began to use the stick for water dowsing like any common water witch. He held two ends of the forked stick in his hands and walked across the fields until the end of the stick dipped down. When the end of the stick pointed toward the ground, there was water beneath the stick, underground. Henry Gross developed his ability, his fame spread, wells were dug, and water was found where his stick

---

[3]Garrett, Eileen J., *Adventures in the Supernormal,* Paperback Library, Inc., New York, 1968, Garrett Publishers Inc., 1949.

[4]Roberts, Kenneth, *Henry Gross and His Dowsing Rod,* Doubleday & Company, Inc., Garden City, New York, 1965.

indicated water. As his ability and fame grew, Kenneth Roberts tested Gross' occult stick with unusual experiments in locating underground water. Gross was found to be a very reliable water dowser. Later, Gross developed the unique technique of simply asking the stick a question which could be answered either yes or no, such as "Is there water on Mr. Smith's farm?" If the stick dipped, it signified yes, and if it remained stationary, it signified no. Using this interesting oracular technique of merely asking his mystic stick questions, Henry Gross located water in Bermuda from a map! After he had located the water on the map, Gross was sponsored by Roberts to travel to Bermuda and pinpoint the location of the underground water. Mr. Roberts financed the digging of wells; thus, Bermuda now has a good supply of local fresh water. Prior to Gross' questioning his rod, water was supplied by ships and one well.

Was Gross controlled by a spirit? Was his stick controlled by a spirit? Was there some unknown natural law involved?

There are many water dowsers who will hold a forked stick in their hands, walk over the ground, and say that they have located water. A dowser who was asked to locate water on the writer's property very confidently walked about, and his stick dipped many times indicating streams of water which, of course, couldn't be seen or detected without digging a well. We drove stakes at the best locations. A few weeks later another dowser was asked to locate water using the switch technique. He brought a friend with him who used two common-looking brass rods to locate water.

The brass rods are supposed to cross when over water. Both rods were L shaped with the small end of the L held, one in each hand, with the long part of the L pointing straight ahead as the dowser walked. These simple brass rods were commonly used very successfully for locating underground tunnels in Viet Nam, underground water-pipes, sewer pipes, etc.

These two water dowsers walked very confidently across the lawn, and apparently located water, but it wasn't where the previous water dowser had located the water. They also walked over underground water pipes in the area and none of them "found" water when passing over a water pipe. Since no two agreed on the location of water, some of these dowsers were apparently unreliable.

This personal experiment indicated that some people who claim to have unusual psychic powers may not have occult ability, or the experiment could be another indication that psychic ability is erratic. It is difficult to tell who has unusual powers and who has an unusual imagination.

A reliable water dowser may receive information on underground water by an ESP signal to his brain which unconsciously moves his hands and arms to allow the stick to dip or rods to turn. The successful water dowser is a person who probably receives information about underground water from the psychic universal broadcast system.

He Sat on Air

Many unusual stories come out of India where monks in monasteries spend much of their life meditating and developing preternatural abilities. These monks seem to have their own communication network, because one man who was investigating their powers arrived unannounced at a monastery to find they were expecting him, although they had no telephones, radios, or other means of communicating with the outside world. One of the monks of this monastery specialized in communication, and he had telepathically communicated with another monk in another monastery who told him that this man was coming to investigate their unusual abilities. In this remote monastery, another monk had developed the occult P-K ability of sitting on nothing. There is a magician's trick which appears to do the same feat. However, this monk was carefully investigated by passing objects completely under the monk and checking all around him. Chickens even ran beneath him as he sat on nothing in the courtyard. The monk explained in detail how he levitated. He imagined that there was one cubic yard of air in front of him, then he imagined that the cubic yard of air was solid. After this mental preparation, he said it was easy to climb up the side of the cube of air and sit on it.

Very simple, but it didn't work for the investigator—possibly because he could not suppress the conscious, logical mind, which said it can't be done, so that he could not generate the ESP signal which could have linked him with universal intelligence, who could have supported the investigator by the motion of the molecules of air and/or the molecules of his body. (As a crude example, a helicopter is supported by the motion of molecules in the air and the motion of molecules in the rotor.)

Thought Travel

Eileen Garrett[5] performed a most unusual experiment in thought travel for the American Society for Psychic Research in New York. In this experiment, she was told to contact a physician by ESP in Newfoundland. She had not visited in the home of the doctor, nor had she met him. When she "turned on" her telepathic communication, she quickly found herself in the physician's house, where she was able to sense all of the smells, scenes, and feelings as if she were physically present. In transcendentally visiting the doctor, who was also a psychic, she was sensed by him as being present, although he couldn't see her. She obtained specific information about the doctor which came from beyond her psychic senses, which were sensing those things inside the doctor's house. For instance, he had a bandage around his head, and she shrewdly knew that he had been in an accident and understood the details of the accident without him explaining this to her. Several objects had been laid on the tables within the doctor's home for her to detect and describe to those who were conducting the experiment. A couple of note-takers were present to write down the information as she obtained it. A few days after the experiment was conducted, the information arrived in New York by mail from the doctor in Newfoundland, telling how he had conducted the experiment from his home, and the names of objects and details of the various tests. He didn't mention his accident, but in answer to a letter of inquiries, he explained the details, which were in complete agreement with Eileen Garrett's story. Eileen apparently tuned to the universal storehouse where all knowledge is stored, and collected only that pertaining to the experiment. Garrett's account of telepathic travel is only one of many of this type.

---

[5] Garrett, Eileen J., *Adventures in the Supernormal,* Paperback Library, Inc., New York, 1968, Garrett Publishers, Inc., 1949.

Travel by thought is acceptable to Rev. Billy Graham. He stated in the September, 1969 issue of *Decision:*

> I have the feeling that we shall be able to travel in heaven. How fast? Now this is my private speculation; it is not in the Bible. But what is the fastest way to travel somewhere today? By thought! You think it, and you are there. Perhaps we shall be able to think our way through the universe, serving God as ambassadors to other celestial bodies, because we are actually the sons of the Living God Who runs this whole creation. That's incredible, it's impossible to believe, but the Bible teaches that we are the sons of God.

Teleportation Moved a Picture

An unusual story was told about Abdul Oab by Keith Ayling.[6] Abdul was the head man of an Arab village where Captain Dubois had cured an epidemic of diphtheria by inoculation. Abdul explained that since these inoculations had almost stopped the spread of the disease, faith could cause continued healing, and their remaining sick people would also be quickly cured. Abdul proclaimed to Dubois that faith could do anything! Of course Dubois, a medical officer, was somewhat skeptical, but Abdul quickly demonstrated one exercise of faith by turning mineral water into one of the finest champagnes. The captain considered this a conjuring trick. And then Abdul performed a real feat. He transferred a picture which was in the captain's home in Paris into the captain's hands in Arabia. The captain examined the picture, checked it carefully, and found that there was no illusion–it was real!

In the meantime, back in Paris, the police didn't find this event very amusing. The picture had been reported missing from the captain's home, and the police were trying to locate it. Abdul kept the picture 48 hours and then, as mysteriously as it left, it was returned to the captain's home. This seemingly wild story of teleportation was reported by the Paris police, the French newspapers, and *The London Times.*

---

[6]Editors of *Fate Magazine, The Strange World of the Occult,* Paperback Library, Inc., New York, 1968, Clark Publishing Company, 1959.

Thought Commands

Astounding experiences and a unique philosophy were related to me by Bill Davis, an aerospace engineer. He and a few others, interested in the occult, in Huntsville, experimented with ESP and other psychic phenomena for several years. Their group found that under hypnosis a person's ESP ability improved tremendously. They also improved their ESP ability and performed many interesting experiments.

One experiment was transmitting a psychic request to another person who was not informed that an experiment was being conducted. Bill and his brother transmitted an ESP command to individuals, urging them to phone them, and many calls came in. One person (a recognized psychic) who had received this impression to call Bill, asked him not to transmit because it interfered with her work. This aroused Bill's curiosity about how strong a signal his brother, who was a better transmitter than he, could send out. He asked his brother to transmit as strong a signal as possible to a secretary who had psychic ability and request that she call Bill. Very soon he received a call from the secretary, who complained of a sudden violent headache and an urgent need to call Bill. During the next four or five hours, Bill received phone calls from acquaintances all over the U.S. who felt a need to call him. So, apparently the signal to the secretary also reached many others much farther away than she was.

Bill has a theory that all behavior, psychic, psychological, moral, and physical, follows a basic simple equation, $\frac{M}{T^2}=\frac{F}{S}$, where M = mass, T = time, F = force, and S = length. Each term is a tensor (any value in any direction). Let us label this equation the "Universal Equation of Truth." From this equation, we can easily derive such common equations as F=MA, $E=MC^2$, etc. The equation can also apply to the ESP signal, P-K, religious concepts, and all equatable relationships in the physical and the spiritual realms. Billy feels that the equation shows the oneness of God. By moving all factors to one side of the equation, they equal "force," God, or Everything equals God.

Automatic Writing

Probably the most carefully documented case of automatic writing, a special form of P-K, is *The Case of Patience Worth.* This book was published in 1934 by Dr. Walter Franklin.

Automatic writing is accomplished when the individual suppresses the conscious mind so that it does not control the hand which holds the pencil. The automatic writing is, theoretically, controlled by a spiritual being who controls the subconscious mind which moves the hand, and a person writes the information without the conscious knowledge of the writer being involved in the process.

Mrs. John H. Curran automatically wrote the story of Patience Worth. She was a medium who had only a very meager education. When she began writing, she had never traveled outside the mid-western United States. Through a strange accident Mrs. Curran began to pick up messages from a mysterious Patience Worth, who claimed to be a young woman of English birth who had come to America in the 1600's. Mrs. Curran had left school after graduating from the eighth grade. She studied voice in Chicago where she attended and played the piano at a spiritualist church where her uncle was the minister. She had attended Sunday School at Protestant churches as a child, but apparently the Protestant teachings, which forbid communicating with spirits, didn't make much of an impression on her. She seemed to have little interest in history, the Bible, or in psychic phenomena. Her first experience with Patience Worth was on July 8, 1930. As Mrs. Curran and some of her neighbors were playing with the occult Ouija Board, she gradually obtained smoother reception. She was told by Patience, who used an Archaic English language, that she had lived in the 1649-1694 period.

Mrs. Curran continued to communicate with the strange spirit of Patience Worth until finally, instead of the slow and tedious process of letters being spelled out on the Ouija Board, Mrs. Curran could see letters in her psychic mind. After this, instead of letters, she began to see words and, finally, the words developed into fascinating scenes in her mind. As this peculiar information came to Mrs. Curran, it was written down, automatically, exactly as received. Complete booklength stories were dictated by Patience Worth to Mrs. Curran. These stories are: *The Sorry Town, The Fool and the Lady*, *Hope Trueblood*, and *The Merry Tale*. She also received many poems from Patience.

The amazing progress of Mrs. Curran from Ouija Board to writing the messages from Patience Worth automatically is phenomenal. Her progress is another indication that the subconscious mind can improve psychic communication ability with the spirit world. Her experience in developing automatic writing is very similar to that of many others who have begun by practicing on a Ouija Board, or other occult device, and gradually progressed to automatic writing or speaking. As Patience Worth states it, "Some of those who are living do seek to communicate in certain cases with those who are not living, and then sometimes messages between the living and dead are possible; however, many messages from the dead are never received because the living do not really try to receive them."

Unusual P-K Mental Powers

Possibly, the method used by Mrs. Curran can be used successfully by many people. Her method can apparently obtain messages from the spirit world, and if the messages come from higher intelligent beings, then there can be great improvements in our way of living in a very short period of time. It would seem from Mrs. Curran's experience that the primary method of improving our contact with this higher life is to be less reluctant to try communicating with the spirit world and simply have more faith that contact is possible. There is a warning, however, for each person who tries to communicate with the spirit world! We should test the spirits by assuring ourselves that they give us factual information in agreement with the teachings of the great Masters. If the spirits do not recognize Jesus as the son of God, we should shun them.

It is always advisable to talk seriously with God and listen to the Holy Spirit and let him help arrange the contact with spirits. However, since there is no better contact than the Holy Spirit, or God, we are safest in communicating only with Him. When we communicate with other spirits, because there may be various levels in the spirit world, we may contact a spirit, at random, who is at one of the lowest spirit levels, who may not have accurate information. In fact, contact with some spirits can be harmful; whereas, if we seek to use the methods of contact taught in the Bible—i.e., speaking to God using the Holy Spirit, with Jesus as a mediator—we can reach the highest level where information will be completely accurate. In addition, we shall not receive information which is harmful to us, because the Holy Spirit judges what is best for us.

P-K Developed a Visible Form

Vadim David Neel[7] tells about an unusual power of the mind which is almost unbelievable. She claims to have produced a thought form which could be seen. She did this by carefully imagining a certain type of person. She chose the form of a monk who was short, fat, and of the innocent, jolly type. She followed some prescribed thought concentrations and other rites which after a few months produced a phantom monk. The monk developed gradually and finally assumed a very life-like appearance. It is interesting to note that she ran into one unexpected problem when she left her apartment to go on a trip. The monk who had been present in the apartment went with her. In fact, from the time he was formed, the monk was her shadow; he stayed with her continually everywhere she went. Some other people could also see the monk, because a herdsman who brought her some food one time thought the monk was a live lama. She realized that she could have created her own hallucination, that he really didn't exist, but it was interesting to note that others also saw the weird materialization. Naturally, she could have had some psychic communication between the hallucination in her mind and the mind of the other individual but this also implies supernormal human ability.

Some Tibetans have an explanation for this phenomenon. They think that there actually is a material form brought into being by concentrated thought. Other Tibetans feel that this is simply an aberration brought on by strong suggestion in the creator's own mind. They theorize that he impresses this suggestion on the minds of others, causing them to see the aberration. With either possibility, the Tibetans assume some strange powers at work.

Eileen J. Garrett[8] also believes in supernatural powers. She said, "I still believe there is an unexplained source of information within mankind which is automatically drawn upon in moments of deep need and emotional stress. The significance of these energies cannot be overlooked, and while I shall expect many setbacks in

---

[7]Neel, Vadim David, *Magic and Mystery in Tibet,* Claude Kendall, Publisher, New York, 1963.

[8]Garrett, Eileen J., *Adventures in the Supernormal,* Garrett Publications, Inc., New York, 1949, p. 161, Paperback Library Edition.

such a study, I feel that in this age of intellectual unrest, any road that promises to throw more light on the question of man's heritage and survival is worth long years of sustained research efforts." Her statement about a "source of information" seems to agree with the concept of a universal storehouse of knowledge and power, which could materialize a monk or cause people to think they see a monk.

Psychic Powers Change Lives

Probably the most unusual and least understood strange power of the mind is that which can completely change a person's life.

The regenerate person is often portrayed as the drunkard, criminal, gambler, or child-beater who suddenly has a change of heart, starts going to church, and becomes a model parent and good citizen. He makes a drastic improvement in his life and many people wonder what caused the change. The regenerate man could also be a young person who has always been good, but he decides to start accepting as a standard of being good what he thinks universal intelligence wants rather than what his parents want. This person portrays little if any change in his behavior when he begins communicating with God, but he is still a new creature because he is talking to universal intelligence.

What is the source of power to change the attitudes and outlook of a man? Is that power within his own mind or is it power from outside of his mind, which mysteriously comes through to change his way of thinking?

Jesus expresses this very unusual mental change which can occur in a person in the following verses:

> Jesus answered and said unto him, Verily, verily, I say unto thee, Except a man be born again, he cannot see the kingdom of God. Nicodemus saith unto him, How can a man be born when he is old? Can he enter the second time into his mother's womb, and be born? Jesus answered, Verily, verily, I say unto thee, Except a man be born of water and of the Spirit, he cannot enter into the kingdom of God. That which is born of the flesh is flesh; and that which is born of the Spirit is Spirit. Marvel not that I said unto thee, Ye must be born again. The wind bloweth where it listeth, and thou hearest the sound thereof, but canst not tell whence it cometh, and wither it goeth: so is every one that is born of the Spirit. *John 3:3-8*

A person who has been born again is a new creature, and the power that was able to transform him into a regenerate man will gently urge him to seek the guidance and leadership of the Holy Spirit in all of his activities. He will be developing his mind to acquire even greater powers as the universal energy intelligence is channeled through him. If he does sincerely seek out and follow the teachings set forth by Jesus, he can possess within his lifetime those powers and capabilities, and even greater powers, than those exercised by Jesus. However, note carefully how the most powerful of all humans, Jesus, used his powers! Note carefully the fantastic control exercised by him in not using his powers to save his own life!

The regenerate man should be able to do more than impose poor images on photographic film, move objects with the powers of the mind, heal the sick, cleanse the lepers, make the blind to see, find water underground, sit on air, know what is going on in another part of the world or in another person's mind, be able to transport objects from one location to another, receive direct messages from the higher intelligence which can be transcribed to paper—he should be able to channel the power that he has in his mind (the knowledge he has of what is required to transform a life) to another person who can also be transformed!

Psychic Powers Helped a Widow Gain Wealth

Powers from the psychic world moved objects and helped a mother gain wealth. When Pat Desilvio's[9] husband died, leaving her with three small children to raise, her world seemed to fall apart. If it had not been for some latent psychic powers which she tapped, she probably would have been a complete failure instead of the successful person she became.

Pat had first discovered her unusual psychic powers as a child while visiting the home of a medium with her aunt. While with the medium, Pat went into a trance and was able to transmit much information to her aunt and others who were present.

Pat continued to develop her peculiar ability to direct psychic forces until the time of her marriage to Louis Desilvio.

---

[9] Suzy Smith, *Widespread Psychic Wonders,* Ace Publishing Corporation, New York, N.Y., 1970.

However, since Louie had no interest in the strange world of psychic phenomena, Pat discontinued the use of her occult talent until circumstances required that she again tap this higher source of power.

During the happy 12 years of their marriage, Louis Desilvio built up a furniture business, which had their apartment over it, but his main interest was his prosperous trucking business.

After Louie's death, Pat continued living in the apartment, and began running the furniture store and the trucking business. Pat was very uncertain of the future, not knowing who to turn to for help in her muddled affairs—then the first of many unexplainable events occurred.

Strangely enough, it was Betty, the 19-year-old baby sitter who experienced the first weird psychic occurrence that heralded Louie's continued interest in his family. Late one night she heard footsteps in the kitchen, and upon investigation found no one. As she entered one room the sound of the steps would move to another, but it was obvious that they were not made by a living person.

Pat's first psycho-kinetic experience came one day at noon while eating lunch with Carol, Louie's daughter by another marriage. When they arose from the table to return to the store for the afternoon's work, a lamp shade mysteriously lifted up and sailed across the room. There was not the slightest breeze to have disturbed the shade and no logical explanation for the unnatural occurrence. Betty and Carol were frightened out of their wits, but Pat immediately sensed that in some unexplainable way Louie was responsible for what had happened, and she felt calm for the first time since his death.

Shortly after this first manifestation of a psychic force moving matter, Louie again made contact. While Carol and Pat were engaged in setting each other's hair, a timer on the stove began to ring of its own accord. They turned it off three times, but each time it would begin to ring again. This was certainly peculiar behavior for a buzzer which had never worked from the time the stove was new.

On another occasion, Betty heard footsteps and the sound of someone opening the refrigerator when no one was in the room.

There were many experiences of psycho-kinesis associated

with Louis Desilvio's continued interest in his family. There were doors which had been closed and checked that were mysteriously opened, and lights that came on and went off of their own accord. Once Louie's voice warned Pat that their two youngest children were in danger, and once he appeared to Pat's sister who had come to work for her.

In one especially vivid dream, Louie told Pat that she would find a piece of property on which to build the home they had dreamed of while he was still alive. He was very explicit, even to the point of drawing a picture of a very peculiarly shaped lot on which she should build the house. Pat was not particularly surprised when some property near the trucking business was offered for sale. The lot had the same unusual shape as the picture which Louie had given her in the dream.

Pat purchased the property and built a home, which she felt Louie shared with her and their children. She had an office in the house for the trucking business which continued to prosper.

Pat felt her success was a result of Louie's continued interest, as shown by psycho-kinetic forces and other psychic manifestations, giving her the courage to go on with the trucking business. She followed the simple technique of accepting the available psychic powers, which gained much happiness for her and her children.

8. THE THEORY OF PSYCHIC PHOTON EMISSION CONTROL

Since we know a power is channeled from the universal energy intelligence to the minds of some Homo sapiens, let's consider in detail how this may be accomplished.

There is possibly one natural law for all psychic phenomena. This natural law, called P-K, has various forms which have been illustrated in previous chapters. If P-K abilities follow natural laws in accomplishing so many unusual feats, how these laws function has not been discovered by the scientists, who are searching farther and farther into the vast universe and deeper and deeper into the inner structure of the atom's mysterious nucleus.

The Smallest Solar System

The elusive atom has never been seen but it has a classical representation which resembles our solar system, much of which we can see without a telescope. The atom's center is the nucleus, comparable to the sun in the solar system, and around the atom's nucleus orbit electrons, comparable to planets orbiting the sun.

Proceeding from this general comparison to the actual detailed characteristics of the atom, the comparison is not valid because the electrons are not solid material, but negative charges of electricity, and the nucleus which has solid material has a positive electrical charge. Where the planets are bound to the sun by gravitational forces, the electrons are bound to the nucleus by electro-magnetic binding forces.

The hydrogen atom has the simplest atomic structure. It has only one orbiting electron and a nucleus of one proton.

The next more complex atom is helium, which has two electrons in its orbital shell and two protons and two neutrons in the nucleus. The helium atom's electron shell, holding only two electrons, is full and will hold no more. The next electron shell of a heavier element (neon) will have a maximum of eight electrons in its outer shell. In the more complicated atoms, there are more electrons and more shells, and more protons and neutrons in the nucleus. Again, comparing an atom to a solar system, the more complicated elements have a larger "sun" and more "planets" in more orbits. Where a solar system normally has only one planet in any one orbit, an atom has several electrons in an orbit (shell), yet the electrons are not in exactly the same orbit because they could collide. They are slightly displaced from each other. Electrons have a precessing orbit in the same manner as planets have a precessing orbit. Precession is the gradual rotation of the orbital plane about the nucleus until the total path of the electrons in an orbit forms a complete shell. Precession is continually repeated over and over. The electrons remain in one energy level within a shell because of the quantity of energy contained in the electron. If the electron receives additional energy in the form of light or photons, it will jump to a higher energy level. If it receives sufficient energy, it will leave the orbit completely and become a free electron somewhat equivalent to a shooting star or comet which no longer falls in orbit about a sun. An orbiting electron, each time it receives a photon, or one particle of light, will gain energy and jump to a slightly higher orbit or energy state. Each time it emits a photon, for some reason, it will drop to a lower energy state.

All atoms within normal materials are in equilibrium and receive exactly the same number of photons as they emit during a specified period of time. This is one reason why normal objects in a room remain at the same temperatures even though the objects do not touch. A light bulb, before you throw the switch, is at the same temperature as everything in the room, and the light bulb doesn't radiate visible light. It is reflecting some light which permits it to be seen. When you throw the light switch, electricity heats the filament, which gives off light because the electrical energy forces the electrons to a higher energy level, and they give off a tremendous number of photons of light as the electrons drop back to lower levels. Electricity is a flow of free electrons through a wire. When electricity flows through a filament, the flowing electrons supply heat to the filament because of the resistance to the movements of electrons, and the friction thereby created heats the wire. The filament is composed of atoms also having electrons in orbit, and it is the electrons in orbit in the filament which give off light and not the free electrons. When hot, the filament is not at equilibrium with its surroundings; therefore, it is emitting photons—and many more than it is receiving.

Another object in the room, for example a pencil, is composed of many atoms, and each atom has many electrons in orbits and each electron is constantly emitting photons or small light particles. While the pencil is constantly emitting photons, the electrons in the pencil are also absorbing photons. There are exactly the same number of photons being absorbed as are being emitted during a minute's time or during an hour's time, unless the temperature of the pencil is changed. If the pencil is heated, it will be absorbing more photons than it is emitting during the time it is being heated.

A scientific mystery is the reason for the emission of a photon or the absorption of a photon which results in the change of energy level of an orbiting electron. It is known that energy in the form of photons can be added to an atom, but if the atom is left alone, it will return to its normal state again by emitting photons. How and why electrons absorb and emit photons is not understood.

The Laser as Controlled Photon Emission

The operation of the laser is one method of controlling the emission of photons from materials. This is accomplished by transmitting a very high-energy photon pulse through a gas which is sensitive to a single frequency of light. As high energy photons pass through the gas, it emits many, many more photons. The laser operates on the principle that a high-energy photon passing near an electron will pull from that electron another photon of the same frequency traveling in the same direction. This cascade effect of each photon producing other photons results in an extremely brilliant flash of light when the laser is pulsed. The laser operation demonstrates one basic method for producing the emission of photons from a material by rapidly shooting high-energy photons near electrons.

Another characteristic of the photon emitted from the atom is its frequency. In the visual spectrum, we "see" the different frequencies as different colors, although the colors are not actually produced as a pure frequency but are apparently produced as differences of frequencies. If photons do not have a frequency in the visible spectrum, the photons are invisible to the human eye but can be detected with special instruments.

Self-Induced Transparency–Invisible?

Research with the laser has produced an unusual effect where the light from a pulse laser is able to pass through an object that is normally opaque to light. A scientist at the University of California in Berkeley, Dr. E.L. Hahn,[1] has succeeded in producing self-induced transparency with pulsated light. He reported this experiment to a meeting of the American Physical Society held in Washington in the spring of 1967.

Considering the theory of how atoms have electrons which can absorb or release light, Hahn says that ordinary incoherent light, having many frequencies, is normally absorbed in an opaque material. This incoherent light transfers its energy of vibration to the target atoms or electrons before it penetrates very far into the material. Hence, the energy of the light beam has been given up to the atoms; it cannot return to the light beam again, but the energy is simply reradiated in all directions from those atoms which absorb it. Now in the case of the laser, which is a single frequency with short bursts of extremely brilliant light, the beam is so intense that it overcomes atomic friction, which means that the

[1]Hahn, E.L., *Scientific American,* June, 1967.

atom's electrons, at first, momentarily absorb light energy, but the electrons will not hold the photons and shortly return the photons to the laser beam.

These photons continue traveling in the same direction. Hahn thinks that this momentary absorption and re-emission of the photons occurs because the extremely brilliant single frequency beam caused the electron and the atom to be set in a cooperative motion which synchronizes with the single frequency light beam vibration.

Hahn said that so far he has only observed this particular phenomenon in insulators, and not in metals or conductors. He also believes that this same effect could be obtained with radio waves, which are simply a different frequency of photon energy, even though radio waves are more readily absorbed than light waves. He has several ideas for other possible uses for this particular phenomenon of the laser.

Far from this sound, scientific discussion of the laser is a story told by Dr. Daniel Fry[2] who said he rode in a UFO in 1950. He said a section of the UFO was made transparent to light by a beam from inside the craft. The beam converted the visible light to x-rays to pass through the metal wall, and then converted them back to light frequencies after traversing the metal hull. His story sounds a little like Dr. Hahn's research results with the laser beam.

Additional research with the laser could lead to some very interesting information about how ESP, or the communication channel of the psychic mind, could be used for producing the emission of photons from matter and controlling P-K. Research revealing how to trigger the release of photons mentally is not such a ridiculous possibility, since there is quite a bit of evidence that at various times minds have been able to move objects and perform other functions, which could be explained if higher intelligence is able to control the emission of photons from matter.

Flames Produce Sounds

Thousands of years ago, a higher intelligent being possibly used a method of controlling the emission of photons from a bush

[2] Fry, Daniel, *The White Sands Incident,* Best Books, Inc., Louisville, Kentucky,

to produce light and a voice to speak to Moses. The well-known account of the Angel of the Lord who spoke to Moses from a burning bush is given in *Exodus 3:2-4*.

> And the angel of the Lord appeared to him in a flame of fire out of the midst of a bush: and he looked, and, behold, the bush burned with fire, and the bush was not consumed. And Moses said, I will now turn aside, and see this great sight, why the bush is not burnt. And when the Lord saw that he turned aside to see, God called unto him out of the midst of the bush, and said, Moses, Moses. And he said, Here am I.

The physical principle which could be used to produce sound from the flame has been demonstrated by scientists[3] at the United Technology Center in early 1968. There, scientists discovered how to use a flame as a high fidelity loudspeaker. They made this discovery while doing research on underwater sound generation. The three scientists involved in this discovery were Wayne Babcock, A.G. Cattaneo, and K.L. Baker. During a brainstorming session, they came up with the possibility of combining electrical and thermal energy and producing sound. They set up an experiment in which a tape recorder plus an amplifier was attached to an ordinary acetylene torch. Imagine their amazement upon hearing the flame of the torch reproducing sound from the tape recorder. They hastily conducted several other simple tests to be certain that they were not imagining that they were hearing things.

Their original work began in mid-1966, and since then much additional research has been conducted. In early 1968 they were producing sounds from a flame under a variety of conditions, yet even after two more years of research, the scientists were unable to determine how the flame produced sound.

An interesting fact about this type of loudspeaker is that the sound is produced omni-directionally, that is, in all directions from the flame. This could be particularly useful in an auditorium or even outside, where you want the sound to be reproduced equally in all directions. The present practice is to use several loudspeakers pointing in various directions to cover a circle around the speaker. Another item of interest is that the flame produces an extremely high-fidelity sound; even though the sound may be a

---

[3] Marshall Star, *Sound-Producing Flame Discovered,* Huntsville, Alabama, January 10, 1968.

high frequency, the flame faithfully reproduces it. In a normal speaker, it is difficult to produce high frequency sounds because the diaphragm must move as the sound is produced, and it cannot faithfully move fast enough for the high frequencies.

Babcock and associates feel that this phenomenon of a flame producing sounds would be very useful in developing very high-speed information transmission systems and super-fidelity loud-speakers. Another practical application was the monitoring of sounds from extremely hot areas, such as the inside of a liquid rocket engine while it is firing. They actually made recordings of the inside of a rocket engine while it was firing.

Another discovery the researchers made is that a small flame readily picks up sounds from a considerable distance. Eavesdroppers could, with a small electronic device installed in a flame, pick up the sound of a distant speaker.

United Technology Center has conducted extensive research to see if there were any other experiments or information pertaining to the effects of sound on flame. They were pleased to find information on some work which has been done dating back as far as 1858, but they said no one ever discovered that flames produce sounds. They did not report other findings.

Based on the quotation from *Exodus,* Moses was aware that a flame could produce a sound thousands of years ago, and apparently some highly intelligent beings made a flame and used it to produce a sound at that time. Again, we find a mentally stimulating, fascinating situation in which, today, we discover scientifically an explanation of how something was accomplished thousands of years ago, apparently by higher intelligent beings. These advanced beings who produced the burning bush may have done so by releasing sufficient photon energy to be visible to Moses, causing the bush to have the appearance of burning without being consumed, and then they used the flame as a speaker.

Ten Miners See Without Light

Bill Shimmer[4] relates how miners who were trapped in a mine by a cave-in either had collective hallucinations or saw light

---

[4] *Fate* Editors, *The Strange World of the Occult,* Clark Publishing Co., 1959, New York, Paperback Library Edition, 1968.

and figures in the cave during a period of pitch blackness. These miners, who were trapped 390 feet underground, claimed that they saw light, but it was a weird bluish light, sort of like steam. They reported that the whole area was filled with this blue light and they could see shadows. Some of the light would appear from a very small area like a match head and then spread until it filled the entire room. One miner thought that it was a soft light, but it was bright enough for him to read his watch. He also had sufficient light to take care of one of his injured miner friends. Another one of the group described it as a bluish light which was there continuously. He also said the light was bright enough so that he could see his watch, but it had no apparent source and filled the entire area.

These miners were entombed for 14 days. They either had hallucinations or saw many other things, including a white marble stairway which seemed to lead up to the roof of the mine. They also claim that they saw three men who were ruggedly handsome, about 6' 3" tall with bronze colored skins and slightly pointed ears. They described them as having thin lips, normal eyes, and their physical appearance was similar to football players. Shimmer obtained his information from interviews with the miners.

This is an extremely weird, unusual story, and we may be so skeptical that we completely reject its validity; however, something happened, either in the mind or collective minds of the miners, or something physical happened in the mine which the miners saw. Could these same higher intelligent beings who produced the flaming bush for Moses also have produced a bluish form of light and caused themselves to be visible. If higher intelligences did perform these feats, they could have done so by controlling the emission of photons from the air in the mine. The bluish light which looked a little like steam could have been glowing of the air itself. The air contains molecules, and if there was an intellectual, controlled emission of photons from the air of the correct wave length, blue light could have been provided. These strange men could have been seen, either because they were physically present in the mine after passing through the ground, by creating bodies for themselves from materials in the mine, or because they controlled the emission of photons so as to produce an image of themselves, similar to a movie projector producing an image on a screen. Such unusual events would seem possible if some higher intelligence controls the emission of photons.

Another explanation for "seeing" objects in the dark has been proposed by Gerald Oster.[5] He has studied phosphenes, which are bright spots or patterns occurring when a person has been subjected to prolonged visual deprivation. He thinks "phosphenes may account for the 'illuminations,'" the visions or the experience of "seeing the light" reported by religious mystics meditating in the dark; they are the "prisoner's cinema" experienced by people in dark dungeons; they may well constitute the fact behind reports of phantoms and ghosts.

Phosphenes can easily be produced by closing the eyes and pressing the eyeball or waiting until patterns begin to appear. Phosphenes have long been recognized by the mystics as an indication of being tuned into the psychic realm. Phosphenes can explain some of the mysterious sights which have been seen, but many others remain a mystery.

Psycho-Kinesis by Control of Photon Emission

Eileen J. Garrett[6] claims to have seen objects being moved or moving under no apparent forces. She said she saw a bunch of lilacs thrown across a central table, along with a number of telltale bells, during a test where psychics attempted to move objects. She has seen an ectoplasmic hand that resembled a human one show itself in space and grasp a handkerchief. She also saw a 112-pound table lifted to the ceiling of the room and there hang suspended until at last it fell and was broken apart when it hit the floor. These psycho-kinetic manifestations were performed under test conditions at South Kingsington, London. The test results have been published by Harry Price.[7]

Bernstein[8] is also a believer in psycho-kinetics. He feels that

---

[5]Oster, Gerald, "Phosphenes," *Scientific American,* February, 1970.

[6]Garrett, Eileen J., *Adventures in the Supernormal,* Paper Library Edition, New York, 1968.

[7]Price, Harry, *Confessions of a Ghost,* Hunter Putnam and Company, London, 1926.

[8]Bernstein, Morey, *The Search for Bridey Murphy,* Pocket Books, Inc., New York, 1956.

data which have been collected in dice throwing tests, conducted at Duke University, are strongly suggestive of a power wherein the mind can control matter. It was noted that the dice throwers' ability to obtain the desired score would fall off rapidly from time to time in a manner which indicated that there was a loss of mental control over the dice (or statistical factors). The changes or declines in his control have a definite pattern far exceeding any expected statistical changes. Odds, he felt, were better than a million to one that such patterns of luck would occur. He believes that the fall of the dice was being worked upon by something more than the machines which threw them, and this phenomenon could only be explained by saying that the mind does indeed control a force which can act on matter.

Is Teleportation Possible?

Who has not had dreams of flying? Most people have had many dreams of flying by concentrated effort. The dreams are so realistic that it doesn't seem possible a person shouldn't be able to fly simply by thinking hard enough about flying. In our dreams, at first, we manage just barely to rise off the ground by extreme mental effort. It isn't very clear what we are concentrating upon to lift ourselves, other than a sincere desire to rise above the ground, and we have faith that it can be done. As we continue to concentrate and perform exercises in concentrations, we rise higher and higher above the ground, clearing fences, finally clearing trees, and then soaring majestically through the air far above the lowly creatures on the ground. These dreams of flying leave us with a vague feeling of anticipation, yet confidence that we can fly if we try hard enough.

Just the fact that most people have dreams of flying has a special significance, either psychological or psychic. These dreams could be explained as a mental condition of the subconscious mind where the mind is relaxed and floating freely in its mental pool of activity. The flying dream may occur when the mind is at a specific level somewhere between a light sleep and a deep sleep. It would be interesting to know what type of brain wave is being produced at the time such a dream is occurring, because if the alpha rhythm is present, it may have some unique characteristics connected to the dream of flying which could be related to the alpha rhythm associated with ESP.

Dreams of flying may have a much more significant meaning than just a mental or psychological oddity. Possibly such strange dreams come to us because higher intelligent beings are capable of flying through the air with mental effort, and we could also have the ability to fly, levitate, or teleportate by simply tuning in to the higher intelligent beings who know the principles involved. Dreams could become reality through contact with higher life, who could provide us with the means necessary to fly, possibly by controlling photon emission in our bodies.

One extra-terrestrial being who lived on earth did have the power to fly through the air. Jesus apparently flew to the peak of the temple with the devil *(Matthew 4:5)*. The devil also indicated that Jesus was capable of flying since he said that if Jesus jumped off the temple, the angels (extra-terrestrial beings) would support him so that he would not strike the ground.

And when Jesus left the earth, he rose into the air *(Acts 1:9-11)*. When Jesus arose into the cloud, the spokesman said that he was "taken up." Did he actually fly through the air? Did he have the power of levitation? It appears so. An extra-terrestrial man rose through the air when he left the earth, and possibly the two men with him departed in the same way.

In another story, the Scriptures report that Jesus and Peter walked on water. Walking on water is very similar to flying through the air; therefore, it would appear that we could fly through the air as easily as we could walk on the water, although we can do neither.

Regardless of whether it is walking on water or flying through the air, one natural law, if such exists, could explain both. That natural law would involve a higher intelligent mind controlling the emission of photons from matter. With such a law, each molecule of the feet, hands, etc., of the individual as he rises through the air in an upright position, would become small jet engines.

If each atom emitted photons in a downward direction, the resultant upward force could lift a person, if the force overcame the pull of gravity. According to the theories of radiation pressure, the force exerted by light is a function of the fourth power of the temperature. Therefore, the force exerted by the human body at 98 degrees Fahrenheit would be extremely minute, if the only photons being emitted are triggered by the temperature effects alone. However, the force would be much greater if some signal, other than temperature effects, caused photons to be released as required. The force required to move objects could be photon reaction if a triggering device is available. Instead of photons being used directly to lift the body, the photons could move surface atoms of the body so that they strike the air molecules with a downward blow. This controlled, photon-produced molecular motion could lift a person into the air like the rotor on a helicopter (moving molecules) lifts the helicopter.

If body energy in the form of heat could be converted with 100% efficiency into work to lift the human body, a person produces much more than enough energy to fly. This is based on the maximum rate at which the body burns energy, 3,000 BTU's per hour. Consider as an example a 200-pound man who will rise through the air. If he rises through the air at the rate of about 1 foot per second, the 200-pound man would consume approximately 1,000 BTU's per hour, which is well within the capability of the human body to produce. His energy consumption rate is comparable to a person jumping a rope as high as a foot each jump at a rate of one time per second. This is hard exercise but not beyond the capability of the human body. Therefore, the assumptions are reasonable that the human body can supply sufficient energy to rise through the air.

How UFO's Perform High "G" Maneuvers

UFO's, which have reportedly been seen flying at tremendous speeds, make very high acceleration ("G") turns. They are going in one direction several thousand miles per hour and very quickly make a sharp turn and proceed in another direction. They have also reportedly been seen accelerating from hovering to extremely high velocity in an instant. Based upon many accounts of these types of UFO maneuvers, high "G" maneuvers seem to be a common characteristic of UFO's.

Another UFO story has been told by a New Zealand couple. This story may not have appeared in print since it came to me through a reliable person who talked to the eye-witnesses. This New Zealand couple noticed a UFO, typical saucer shape, in broad daylight, flying toward their house. They observed it in amazement as the UFO flew and maneuvered about, traveling at a very high speed in one direction, then another. There was nothing unusual or phenomenal about the strange maneuvers, except it was a very exciting experience to this couple who had never before seen a UFO. They had an odd feeling of guilt as they watched the unearthly performance, and they were almost afraid to even admit to themselves that they were seeing one of "those things" which so many people had talked about, although many people will not even take a position on the existence of UFO's. While watching the UFO flitting about, they noticed that their neighbors were also standing outside intently scrutinizing the interesting maneuvers of this possible extra-terrestrial vehicle. Since their neighbors were also watching it, they considered it to be, at least, not an hallucination. Afterwards they discussed the UFO with their neighbors, and they all concluded that they must have seen something. This New Zealand couple, like many others, were willing to tell the story only to very select people whom they considered non-critical and would not ridicule them.

If a human being were riding in a UFO and the vehicle performed the high maneuvers that have been so often observed, the human being would be killed. He would be killed in the same manner that a person is killed when his automobile traveling at 60 mph hits a concrete wall.

The body which was traveling at 60 mph must come to a complete rest in a very short period of time. The first portion of the body which contacts some surface, such as the dash of the car will be stopped by the dash, and the remaining molecules of the body will pile up, crushing the forward part of the body. The human being's body will be broken, torn, and damaged beyond repair, and the victim will die.

Let's assume that the higher intelligence beings have a body which resembles ours, but they have each molecule independently controlled by the brain. When their body experiences a high acceleration, the force is applied equally to each molecule. They can withstand sudden vehicle accelerations of hundreds of G's. As they accelerate, the body surface in contact with their vehicle seat will experience the high force. The adjacent molecules of the body will also experience a force of the same magnitude, if each molecule is also accelerated with its own small jet engine by emission of photons in the correct direction. The only change experienced is that molecules which normally release photons in all directions will release photons in one direction as much as is required to counter-balance the force of acceleration.

Another way to visualize effects of acceleration on their bodies is to imagine that the energy utilized to accelerate their vehicles is applied to each atom of the vehicle and all objects within the vehicle. Where our space vehicles have a rocket engine pushing on a structure which then transmits the force to the vehicle and all material within it, their energy source may transmit its force directly to each atom by triggering the release of photons. With each atom having a force applied directly to it, the higher beings can withstand tremendous accelerations up to those forces required to crush a molecule.

The entire vehicle can perform very high G maneuvers by accelerating each atom so that the vehicle and passengers are not crushed due to a piling up of molecules.

Intellectually controlled molecular motion may be used by UFO's to avoid colliding when they meet another object. As a UFO approaches an object, it is not necessary for the entire vehicle to go around the obstruction, but it can avoid the obstruction on an individual molecular basis only. Each molecule of the vehicle can go around the molecules which are in its path. The molecules of the vehicle will perform a rapid zig-zag motion as the vehicle passes through another object. Such molecular motion would not affect the shape of the vehicle because the movement of molecules would be no greater than normal molecular motion. By molecular control, the UFO's could pass through our atmosphere without resistance or noise. They could pass through the entire earth, through an airplane, or another UFO vehicle. The nebulous UFO's may pass through solid objects and not collide with them by maneuvering molecules so that molecules do not collide. As has been suggested previously, some of the UFO's sighted, particularly those which are only lights, may be merely light images projected into the physical world from the psychic world, while others may be solid, physical bodies.

When Jesus passed through the wall of a room *(John 20:19)*, he may have used the technique of moving the molecules of his body so that they avoided molecules in the walls.

Faith-Healing by Moving Molecules

The principle of photon emission control could account for faith-healing by moving and relocating of molecules into a proper orientation. If the human body has a defect, correcting the defect may consist of relocating atoms and molecules to where they belong. They could then resume their normal function. If the body has a chemical imbalance, by maneuvering the molecules to produce proper chemical reactions, re-orienting to the correct chemical balance could be accomplished. For faith-healing to occur, someone must channel the power of a higher intelligence into the person who is to be healed. This is why some medical doctors, who have made a study of faith-healing report that they have observed that it is always necessary for some person to have faith for another to be healed. It is not necessary for the person who is ill to have faith, but some individual must exercise faith. Faith-healing is accomplished by this person, who by faith channels the power of the higher intelligence, or possibly amplifies this power or directs it to the person who is healed. Are healing powers and other powers to perform miracles always available from the higher intelligence? To have this power may require only the establishing of the communication link to the source of power. To connect with this source of power may require that some person have a desire to use that power correctly, for healing a person or performing some other unselfish act which could benefit mankind or some individual. Faith-healing is not always accomplished when a person wishes for another to be healed; faith does not always heal a person even though faith is exercised. But where the person desiring the healing power does not receive it, the higher intelligence gives him a message. This message will usually satisfy the individual who has sought healing power, and he will comprehend an even higher level of God's purpose than healing of a loved one.

No Healing but a Message Was Received

My younger brother, Floyd, who died of cancer when he was 32 years old, knew he had terminal cancer about a year before he passed away. After he knew his condition, he related much of his religious philosophy to me during several discussions. He quit school when he was in the eighth grade, even though he had a high IQ. No special effort was required for him to make very good grades in school. But he had very little ambition; he didn't particularly want to continue his studies even though they required only minor effort. After quitting school, he worked at various jobs, as he grew into a fine specimen of a man, standing over 6' 4" tall and weighing 200-250 pounds. He finally decided on an army career and enlisted as a private. During the time he was in the army, he had several close encounters with death where normally a person would have been killed. One time he was driving an almost brand new '53 Chevrolet car at night and fell asleep at the steering wheel. He didn't know for certain how fast he was driving but he had been traveling at a very high rate of speed prior to falling asleep. He hit a Greyhound bus head-on which was also traveling at a high rate of speed. His car was totally demolished, but he miraculously came through the catastrophe with only minor scratches and bruises.

Another time while Floyd was in the Army, on maneuvers at night, he was driving a tank without lights and could not see where he was going since he had only a small slit to peek through. But he had a lookout, who, with his head protruding from the top of the tank, was trying to see where they were going even though it was very dark. Floyd was given signals of which way to go with the lookout's feet on his shoulders. Although Floyd couldn't see anything obstructing his path, he had the feeling that he should stop the tank, which he did, even though his cohort signaled him to continue. He wasn't satisfied to move the tank until he and the other fellow climbed out of the tank, and walked around in front of it. To their amazement, they discovered that they were on the edge of a cliff. If he had moved the tank a few feet farther, they would have tumbled over the precipice.

In another case, he was bitten by a rattlesnake and could have died, but recovered with apparently no harmful effects. Several times he developed severe pneumonia, became delirious, but recovered.

About two years before the doctors discovered that he had Hodgkin's Disease, he was experiencing some difficulty with fluid accumulating in his lungs.

Doctors had been running tests but could not locate the cause of the problem. Finally, after deciding to operate, they opened his chest to examine his lung cavity for some signs of foreign material which could cause the fluid accumulation. The doctors carefully examined his lung cavity but could not find any abnormal condition, and they were about to conclude their examination when a nurse brought to the doctor's attention a very obscure discoloration on a lung. The doctors removed the spot which was later determined to be a malignant growth. They thought it would have killed him within a short time if it had not been removed. This lung cancer apparently had no connection with the Hodgkin's Disease which was discovered a couple of years later.

After he contacted Hodgkin's Disease, and after it had been diagnosed, he was placed in the Walter Reed Hospital in Washington, D.C. He was there when I talked to him about a year before he died and he expounded upon the message which he had received in regard to his unusual life's story. When he was a youth, he felt that God intended for him to be a preacher, but he rejected God's plan. He had insufficient ambition to become a preacher, and he felt that his narrow escapes from death were messages from God asking him to better utilize his talents. He had always served actively in churches wherever he was stationed. He held church offices and also worked very closely with the army chaplains.

We may think that his church work would be sufficient effort to satisfy God; however, he still did not feel that this was what God intended for him to do. When he was told that he had Hodgkin's Disease, the doctors could not predict how long he would live or whether or not he would die from it. He was told by the doctors that no one had recovered from the disease; although, some people had lived for six or eight years after contracting it. He began taking treatments with drugs and radiation to retard the growth of tumors in his body. He believed that he should continue his education and become a preacher in spite of his condition, so he enrolled at a university in Washington and began taking courses in history.

After my visit with him in Washington, I returned home and didn't have contact with him for several weeks. Later, I discovered that he was in Kentucky where our parents lived, helping his father-in-law cut fence posts and doing other odd jobs. Not many months later he had to return to Washington, D.C. again, because he had become very ill. This time the doctors tried treatments and surgery—but all to no avail, because tumors had progressed too far in his body for the doctors to arrest them.

I went to Washington again to visit him when he was in very critical condition. When I arrived he was already in a semiconscious state and did not readily recognize me, although he did make some sounds which were not understandable. I stayed by his bedside the few nights I was there. One evening I went to bed rather early, around 6:00 p.m., so that I could get some sleep before I went to the hospital at midnight to stay with him. While lying on my bed I began earnestly talking to God, asking Him to heal my brother, in spite of the extent to which the cancer had already taken over his body. I had firm faith that God could heal him, and it only required the faith of one individual for him to be healed even though he was so near death. As I prayed, listening for God to speak, strange things, which had never happened before, began to happen in my mind.

Pictures began to flash into my mind; one of these pictures was very vivid and still stays in my memory as if it were indelibly impressed on it. This is the picture of an individual dressed completely in black. He had on a long garment and a large, wide-brimmed, high-top hat, similar to hats sometimes worn by monks. His face was very calm and benevolent, as he came through a door into a room. He didn't say anything, made no particular motion; however, I had the impression that he was telling me, "We have heard your request, but there is another message for you which is more important. The message is this:" (Now I saw the individual only for an instant, but these thoughts which follow formulated after midnight while I was sitting with my brother.)

A Purpose for Each Person

When each soul comes into this life, he is given certain talents and abilities. He is expected to use these abilities, although he is not forced to use them. If he should not use his talents, he may lose them. In many cases, where a person is serving God, but he is doing far less than he is capable of doing, his life, in effect, is being wasted on earth. Not in the sense of punishment, but in the sense of better use of his talents, he is taken to the spirit universe,

> which may be the next level for intellectual development. If we have been given talents and capabilities on earth which are not used properly, these talents and their possessors may be taken to the psychic realm. We are not punished by death nor are our loved ones punished, although they may have that attitude for some time, particularly if they do not talk to God and have no understanding with Him.

The above message was received in response to my request for God to heal Floyd. It was a message which satisfied me. It was not a message which I felt was the total answer to why he had to die, but it was, nevertheless, a reason in my own mind of why my prayer for faith-healing was rejected.

ICMM for Life

Intellectually Controlled Molecular Motion (ICMM) or P-K may be necessary for life. What starts biological life and what stops biological life is a mystery. Scientists are digging deeper and deeper into the mysteries of life, and they have found that the DNA chain in the chromosomes of an individual determine all the characteristics of each cell of that individual. There is also within this DNA chain, programming signals which determine how each cell will develop and how the adjoining cells are connected with it. When one cell dies, in most cases another one is grown to replace it. This process continues on and on until for some strange reason the reproduction of new cells deteriorates as if the signals become faulty. This is called "aging." Aging behaves like it is a disease in the body of an individual. For each cell to reproduce or to grow, there must be chemical reactions and the moving about of atoms and molecules in the proper orientation for correct cell structure. Thus, each cell is a very complicated molecular structure composed of many long-chain molecules. To build this very complicated cell, a blueprint must be followed. This blueprint is called the DNA chain in the cell. For some unknown reason, the blueprint becomes faulty or defective and the reproduction process becomes imperfect with age. Could it be that higher intelligent beings set in progress an intellectually controlled molecular motion of cells in a person or a living organism? The DNA chain would be the programmer which sends out those signals which in some way release the photons directionally from matter, so that the atoms and molecules are properly arranged to produce another cell. And then old age or aging would be a breakdown of the communication channel between higher intelligence, or maybe higher intelligence merely sets a life in motion like we wind a clock. They place all the necessary energy, signals, and intelligence, into the DNA chain and brains, etc. of the individual or organism for that organism to live a specified period of time. They may no longer interfere or control the life of the individual, and, finally, the brain or the clock runs down and that biological being dies. What if an intelligent being, such as a Homo sapiens, could recontact the source of life and develop a communication channel strong enough, good enough, and accurate enough to continue to channel this natural law of P-K into his body. Would he die?

Eileen J. Garrett[9] claims to be able to see spherical bodies of light around all living objects, flowers, trees, birds, etc. She also felt that these blobs of light contain some kind of "colorstuff" which was being absorbed by the living objects. During the middle of the day, the tiny globules seem to shrink down toward the flowers due to the intense heat of the sun, but in the evenings the spheres were bigger and livelier, seemed to dance and shimmer and be full of life and vitality. She felt that these globs of light were a little akin to laughter. Could she have seen with her psychic mind some representation of the intellectually controlled molecular motion which may be required to keep all objects alive? Or did she see the psychic signal which is responsible for the sensitivity of plants detected by Cleve Backster?[10]

Use of Psychic Photon Emission in ESP

The thinking process of the human brain is not well understood, but some general information is available.[11] For thought processes, the brain produces electrical impulses which originate

---

[9] Garrett, Eileen J., *Adventures in the Supernormal*, Paper Library Edition, New York, 1968.

[10] Backster, Cleve, "Evidence of a Primary Perception in Plant Life," *International Journal of Parapsychology*, Vol. X, winter, 1968.

[11] Lessing, Lawrence, "Inside the Molecules of the Mind," *Fortune*, July 1, 1966.

from electro-chemical processes. From this crude knowledge, it is reasonable to assume that within the brain, billions of atoms are emitting photons as the electrons of atoms are changing energy states. This action of photons can produce electric current flow, as in the photo-electric cell, solar cell, or retina of the eye. For intelligent thought processes to occur when photons are emitted, some logic pattern is required. An example is a T.V. signal to the T.V. set. This signal is totally photons of various frequencies, but the photons are grouped so that the receiver can decipher from the flood of photons, intelligent information. A picture is produced on the screen and sound comes from the speaker. Possibly within the human thinking process are electrical signals which can be produced by the controlled emission of photons.

For a higher intelligence to produce an idea or thought in our minds, he may control the emission of photons in a prescribed pattern within our brain. He could transmit a coded signal similar to T.V. Since some brains are good receivers because of physical characteristics and others only receive under unusual circumstances, the higher beings contact individuals selectively.

All of us can improve reception by following prescribed exercises. I was attempting to follow Scriptural methods when praying for Floyd to be healed, and received a message possibly from a higher intelligence (God) who controlled the emission of photons in my mind.

The brain is composed of about 10 billion neurons or brain cells. Each cell has within it a high concentration of potassium ions, and the cell has on the outside a concentration of sodium ions. When an electrical impulse from one of the five senses hits a neuron, it causes a breakdown of the potential voltage across the neuron, which shoots out a tiny electric current. This signal goes to other parts of the brain where the sensed signal is recognized and/or understood.

Signals also come from within the brain, as well as through our five senses, but what triggers the release of a tiny electric current within the brain is not known. It is possible that the ESP signal triggers the release of a photon which can, in turn, trigger the release of a tiny electric current. The signal which constantly suffuses the brain is the alpha rhythm wave, a steady, low-voltage background signal, which changes pattern with alertness, drowsiness, concentration, and specific sensory excitation.

The alpha rhythm brain wave is related to ESP and to the firing of neurons in the brain. Possibly the alpha rhythm, a systematic firing of neurons, is modified or influenced by the ESP signal.

Another communication medium proposed by T.G. Hieronymus, a famous inventor of mystical machines, is eloptic energy. He feels that eloptic energy uses light rays and magnetic flux lines as a carrier medium, and it's this energy which carries thoughts between persons and messages between beings of our universe. He thinks there may be various frequencies in the eloptic energy band.

Since eloptic energy has not been identified in scientific research, its concept is not recognized by the scientists. This however, does not rule out the existence of eloptic energy, but further research may detect it. Eloptic energy could account for the ESP phenomenon. This idea could also be related to the tachyon theory proposed by Feinberg.[12]

Control of P-K

Technical progress is rapidly increasing because of improved use of our intellectual capability, but how far can we go? Human beings are collectively thinking: they are thinking about tremendous projects such as travel to the moon and other planets; development of high energy sources such as nuclear power; cures for many diseases such as cancer; transplanting of hearts and other organs of the body; and many other intellectual miracles. The human mind is being linked with the computer so that the thinking speed and capacity of the mind is increasing tremendously. The progress in intellectual capability has no known boundaries.

If technical progress leads to development of very sensitive devices which detect the position of the electron in orbit, by detecting the emission of photons the atom could be moved, but much progress is necessary before science reaches this level. If technical progress leads to a means of contacting beings who

---

[12]Feinberg, Gerald, "Particles That go Faster Than Light," *Scientific American*, Feb. 1970.

already know how to move matter, then we could move matter by thought. If everyone could move objects by thought, wouldn't there be chaos because everyone would want to "go his own way"? One object could collide with another, but if there were accurate controls, the controller could cause one object to pass through another, avoiding collisions of atoms. Won't this movement of objects be confusing? The entire earth and all life on it may turn into a plasma of flesh and bones, trees and grass, in which one object is passing through another object. Everything could become mixed most of the time. Would this be an unobstructed universe as described by White?[13]

Over the past several years, many transportation devices have been developed which travel at tremendous speeds, while some transportation devices travel very slowly. One slow transportation system is the human being as he walks along. He is able to think quickly enough while he is walking to stop within one step. Even when running, there is little danger of running into anything if he is alert. As we have become more knowledgeable and have advanced our technology, we can move much faster than a walk. When we move faster than a walk, such as riding a bicycle, we use our intelligence to develop brakes to help us stop faster. We also use our intelligence to travel in areas where we would not be likely to run into people or other objects. When we progressed to automobiles, we built better roads. We restricted people from walking in the roads and horsedrawn carriages from traveling on the road, so there would be less likelihood of collisions. As we progressed on to aircraft and traveled faster, the controls of movement became tighter and more elaborate. We have detailed rules of what can and cannot be done when we move objects through the air. We are proceeding into space, and each time a vehicle is launched, we exercise stringent controls on the exact trajectory it must follow as it leaves the launch pad. We so tightly restrict its trajectory, that if it strays a few degrees, the vehicle is destroyed to prevent it from falling in a populated area and endangering lives. In effect, what we are doing is learning to move objects by thought! We move the objects by intelligence; the intelligence does not direct a signal to the object, but we learn a

---

[13]White, Stewart E., *The Unobstructed Universe,* E,P. Dutton & Co., Inc., New York, 1940.

lot—we learn techniques, we learn capabilities, we learn controls and restraints. We find that our abilities must always be restricted so that we do not harm other individuals. As we continue to learn to move objects at higher and higher speeds, we shall also learn more about how to control and direct these objects by thought. We shall develop more safety measures and precautions and make certain the objects do not interfere with other individuals' rights or endanger lives. Are we progressing intellectually in techniques, controls, and moral issues so that some day when we have complete contact with higher intelligent beings and we can easily move objects simply by thought, we, in turn, will correctly use our new-found powers? Until we have a high degree of moral control, let us be thankful that not many people can move objects simply by thought concentration.

9. BEGINNINGS TO ULTIMATE USES OF PSYCHO-KINESIS

In attempting to be professionally objective, some of this chapter may be considered speculation, although my personal feelings are that it contains ideas which come from the universal mind. Maybe these ideas are partly imagination, but they may have a degree of validity which can justify passing them on to the reader, who can accept those ideas which help him arrive at a logical picture of the universe and reject those which are incompatible with his concepts. In this manner, as millions of people continue to receive some information from the universal mind, the collective concepts of our universe will become nearer and nearer to the truth, if facts are used up before imagination begins.

Probably, primary inaccuracies in my, or in your, concept of the universe will be in areas where our present knowledge is insufficient to allow us to understand the message we are receiving from the energy intelligence. Possibly all universal knowledge is available to us continually on the universal broadcast band, but the only part of this vast wealth of knowledge that we can use is that which our intelligence and knowledge can assimilate. Maybe even control of P-K requires some expansion of our knowledge and/or intelligence before we can make great progress.

What natural laws govern the psychic world, controlling how we can use the powers there, are unknown to us; thus, we are uncertain of how to exercise psychic powers even if we can lay claim to them. As the natural psychic laws are learned, we should be able to more freely perform tremendous feats of P-K.

The Functioning of P-K in the Physical Universe

The universe is extremely impressive because of its vastness, which is beyond the reach of our telescopes and even our imaginations. With radio telescopes, the universe has been observed to extend billions of light years in all directions, but its outer edges have not been found. The universe is estimated to be over 11 billion years old, whereas the earth is only 4.7 billion years old. It contains billions of suns which probably have planets, although the only planets which we are certain exist are in our solar system. With billions of planets in the universe and with many of these older than the earth by billions of years, regardless of how life arrived on earth, it should have existed elsewhere in the universe long before it arrived on earth. The universe has mysterious quasars, "pulsars," supernova, and star galaxies, yet from the cosmological viewpoint, there is no proof of life beyond the earth's atmosphere, unless the discovery, in a meteor, of the basic building block of life, amino acids, constitutes proof.

The Bible, mythology, and history give many accounts of beings on the earth who were believed to be non-human by the ancient writers. These writers called the strange visitors God, gods, angels, sons of God, and unusual men. In addition to Biblical historical accounts, considered reliable by millions of people, many other ancient accounts are given of strange visitors from outside our planet. Using these ancient tales about extra-terrestrial visitors and unconfirmed modern stories, the physical universe seems to be a system of physical living beings, with the Homo sapiens species presently at the level of supreme being on the earth, while there are superior beings outside the earth who visit, oversee, and communicate with us. These superior beings may have reached their intellectual level in the same way that we shall reach their level.

Assuming that superior, extra-terrestrial beings have been around the earth for thousands of years, their presence accounts for the many stories[1] of unusual "clouds" which carry "God" and "angels." These beings would also account for UFO's,[2] the "Chariot of Fire," Ezekiel's visitors, and many others. These superior beings seem to have a transportation system which may be a living system. They may live in these vehicles in space as readily as we live in houses on earth. They may have been working with life on earth for billions of years, helping it advance to a point where earth life can become aware of universal life and communicate with it. Extra-terrestrial beings are mentioned in the Bible in the Garden of Eden (God), in the days of Noah (sons of God), Abraham and Lot, Sodom and Gomorrah (angels, God, and men), when Jesus ascended (two men in white), and in many other stories. These superior beings and their behavior have given us another bit of data to use in arriving at a concept of the universe.

Communication by Telepathy

In the Biblical stories, communication with extra-terrestrial beings was both audible and telepathic. Since the early thirties, reliable research by Dr. Rhine[3] at Duke University and several other research institutions[4] has verified that human beings have a sixth sense which may be the sense for communicating with superior beings. Although communication by telepathy is very common among Homo sapiens, we do not think of it as communication but that of mysteriously knowing facts which are not received through the five senses.

---

[1] Fort, Charles, *The Book of the Damned,* Ace Books, Inc., New York, N.Y., 1941.

[2] Keyhoe, D.E., *Flying Saucers: Top Secret,* G.P. Putnam's Sons, New York, 1960.

[3] Rhine, J.B., Pratt, J.G., et al., *Extra-Sensory Perception After 60 Years,* Bruch Humphries, Pub., Boston, 1966.

[4] Ryzl, M. *Model of Parapsychological Communication,* Sdelovaci Techinka (Czechoslovakian), Patterson AFB, Ohio, 1964.

Sugrue, Thomas, *There Is a River–The Story of Edgar Cayce,* Henry Holt & Co., New York, 1959.

Hansel, C.E.M., *ESP a Scientific Evaluation,* Charles Scribner's Sons, New York, 1966.

Many people have dreams[5] which come true, hunches which are right, women's intuition, recognizing a place that we haven't been in before, etc. Then, a few specially gifted people such as Jeanne Dixon[6] seem to have many correct prophecies. Other unusual people, such as Ted Serios,[7] can impose mental images on photographic film, but research with plants performed by Cleve Backster[8] indicates that all life and possibly non-life communicates or responds as if it is part of a higher living system which sends and receives signals to all matter.

Whether man had better extrasensory perception (ESP) in the past and lost it or is developing it, is unknown,[9] but the evidence indicates that he once had better ESP, and he is slowly regaining what he has lost. During some evolutionary or developmental stage, man was probably given the ability to communicate with his sixth sense much better than he does now, but he apparently lost much of this talent due to non-use. There are many Bible stories which seem to bear this out, but most convincing is the story of Jesus, an extra-terrestrial being who apparently had excellent ESP communication with universal life.

Within the teachings of Jesus there seems to be outlined a method for Homo sapiens to use in improving his contact with superior intelligent beings. This method has, as a pre-requisite to developing communications, a requirement for the awareness of a superior being. If we are aware of a superior being and want to communicate with him, we may be reluctant to contact him because of awe or fear of his power. "What if he became angry at me for some reason? He could eliminate me with a thought." We may realize that a superior being is displeased with many of our childish actions, and we would not be willing to contact him unless we know that he loves us in spite of our behavior. This method which is described for developing contact with energy intelligence contains proof of his love because he loved us enough

---

[5] Freud, Sigmund, *The Interpretation of Dreams*, Random House, New York, 1950.

[6] Montgomery, Ruth, *A Gift of Prophecy*; Morrow Pub., New York, 1965.

[7] Eisenbud, Jule, *The World of Ted Serios*, William Morrow and Co., Inc., 1967.

[8] Backster, Cleve, "Evidence of a Primary Perception in Plants," *International Journal of Parapsychology*, Vol. X, 1968, No. 4.

[9] Hardy, A.C., "Telepathy and Evolutionary Theory," *Journal SPR* 1960.

to die for us–and did. If we realize the magnitude of his interest in us, our fears disappear and we want to communicate with the higher intelligence of the universe. The method taught by Christ can now become effective because we shall try to ask the higher intelligence questions and expect to receive answers.

Communication with a higher intelligence is not as easy as talking to a peer, but our efforts to communicate will be rewarded with improved understanding. The contacts should result in ESP ability similar to Jeanne Dixon,[10] yet we might have even better results, because we may learn what is required of us to perform a useful service to mankind. Improving our contact will result in greater power; however, as is always the case, with greater powers goes the responsibility of greater controls.

The method taught by Jesus for improving communication with the universal mind is one requiring improved moral controls to gain increasing powers. This method requires concern and interest in others.

Complete contact with the universal mind may cause a person to behave as if he is part of the universal mind. This would place him in an unacceptable position among people who could not understand his behavior. The person may be excluded from society by any means considered necessary by society. Even though very few persons, maybe only Jesus, have had complete contact, even those with superior contact have been social outcasts and they have even been killed.

If superior beings are supervising us and ride in "clouds" or UFO's, they may not be able to live among us because we would endanger their existence. Yet superior beings may soon find among Homo sapiens an environment acceptable for their existence so that they can live with us, if we shall continue to improve our psychic ability, including P-K.

The Nature of Universal Life

Universal life,[11] superior beings, may be overseers of planets where new life is developing. New planets may be seeded with life

---

[0]Montgomery, Ruth, *Gift of Prophecy*, Morrow Pub., New York, 1965.

[11]Clark, Adrian V., *Cosmic Mysteries of the Universe*, Parker Publishing Co., Inc., West Nyack, New York, 1968.

by a universal life system. The superior life may use natural laws which can move objects by thought, and they may exist in a zero-dimensional universe,[12] where, in our physical universe, mass is being converted into knowledge by Homo sapiens type beings.

Objects may be moved by thought, using a psychic signal which can trigger the directional release of photons from matter. As photons leave an atom in one direction only, the object containing the atom will move in the opposite direction, or the object can receive a greater force from its environment, such as air, by directing the atoms in the object against air molecules so that each atom strikes air molecules in a direction to lift the object. There is considerable evidence to support this proposal that a natural law exists which allows the movement of matter by thought.

There may be another smaller universal cycle through which the earth and life on it are proceeding. The cycle has no start or end, but for a discussion starting point, we shall begin with superior thinking beings who produce light, a form of electromagnetic radiation. Even inferior Homo sapiens produces light in the form of brain waves when thinking.

Light in the universe may be going through processes which form hydrogen, the simplest atom and the most plentiful in the universe.

Hydrogen condenses into stars which produce heavier elements and planets on which life can exist.

Planets may be seeded with life, which is developed to higher and higher levels until it can convert mass into knowledge. When we learn, we use energy from food to produce knowledge, which may become a part of the universal storehouse of knowledge.

Higher life on a planet will finally communicate successfully with universal life, will become a part of universal life, and will no longer be dependent upon a planet for existence. Their home planet and solar system will burn out and die, but these beings will continue to exist in the unobstructed universe[13] or at some location in the physical universe.

---

[12]White, S.E., *The Unobstructed Universe,* E.P. Dutton and Co., Inc., New York, 1940.

[13]White, S.E., *The Unobstructed Universe,* E.P. Dutton & Co., Inc., New York, 1940.

Universal life existing in universal cloud habitats think, producing light which also continues the cycle in the universe.

This concept of the universe is based upon facts and imagination. But what is the source of imagination? Mankind may be on the verge of contact with universal life, which when accomplished will greatly improve our mode of existence and happiness. The primary obstacle to improved contact is lack of consideration for our fellowman.

When the first astronauts *(Apollo 8)* were making final preparations for their trip around the moon in December, 1968, some people who claimed to be communicating with higher intelligence predicted that the astronauts would be able to communicate much better with higher life while they were outside the earth's environment. This prediction was not verified; but the first moon visitors certainly express concepts indicative of recognizing, if not communicating with, superior beings. The astronauts acknowledged God as creator of the earth and moon during their Christmas season voyage, 1968. Some people in contact with super-intelligence are proposing that the space program is part of a master plan being carried out by the superior universal intelligence.

The Unobstructed Universe

Totally intermingled with the physical universe may be the psychic or unobstructed universe, which seems to be necessary to explain fully ESP, P-K, God, angels, UFO's, and many other things which are observed in the physical universe. The unobstructed universe may be the place of spirit beings who have passed into that realm from the physical universe.

As a being proceeds from the physical to the spiritual, he goes from a point source (as a body we are at one place in the universe) possibly to a distribution throughout the spirit universe. Or when the soul departs this physical world, he may go to the spiritual universe as a system which is everywhere in the spirit universe. It is more likely that the soul does not go from the physical to the spiritual universe, but that the soul is in the spirit and physical universe all the time. When the physical body dies, the soul loses its strong contact with the physical world which the soul has because of the body's five senses, and the soul can then experience more easily the spirit universe. In the spirit world, the soul is a part of all spiritual beings, or the soul communicates with all spirit beings the way one part of our brain communicates with another part. However, souls may each have an identity even more than a part of one's brain has a personal identity. Each soul seems to continue a learning process, the same way that most of our physical lives are devoted to learning processes. In fact, it seems that many times the primary reason for a person's physical death is because he is no longer learning much or as much as he is capable of learning, and with death he goes into the spirit realm where he can continue to learn. Even in the spirit universe there are indications that some spirits are extremely slow learners.

These ideas about the spirit world have been obtained primarily from people who have had contact with discarnate spirits. The ideas have also been formulated from evidence in the physical world gained from studies in scientific fields, and an imagination which ties together the parts and pieces as if the universal mind were guiding me to an explanation of the unexplained.

When I am told by a person that he has seen or talked to a spirit, there is no way for me to verify his story, but in most cases I can determine the integrity of the person. I can assume that the person thinks the story is true based upon his normal honesty. If the story has originated totally within his mind, the mind has a very peculiar behavior which needs to be explored and understood.

In Huntsville, Alabama, many engineers and scientists who work in the aerospace industry and upon military weapons are investigating psychic phenomena. They are aware that very unusual things are happening which have no explanation in science; therefore, they assume that a scientific explanation is possible and search for the answers.

The following true story illustrates a psychic experience of researchers in Huntsville.

Warren York, a young aerospace laboratory scientist in Huntsville, Alabama, has investigated many areas in the psychic realm using sensitive electronic equipment and hypnosis. He used hypnosis to help a lady who was bothered by a spirit identity possessing her mind. After hypnotizing the lady, she said she could see a glow around electrical appliances whether they were on or off, but when they were unplugged she saw no glow. When a magnet was placed near the appliance, she no longer saw a glow.

She could see objects everywhere in the room regardless of their location. With a book between her and an object, she could readily describe the object. She said that she saw all around her in a "knowing" fashion rather than direct vision with her eyes. She never blinked her eyes during the half hour she was hypnotized.

After this initial interesting investigation, York then came to the real reason for hypnotizing her by asking that the possessing spirit identify himself. The spirit said he was William.

When William took control of the lady, she became colder to the touch, and her voice and characteristics changed as if she were another person. She seemed to have difficulty expressing what William wanted to say.

When York asked William when he lived and where, although the information was sketchy, York understood that he lived sometime long, long ago in a grass hut during the time of dinosaurs when all people of that time were dark skinned like Egyptians.

York then took a novel approach and allowed William to ask him questions.

William wanted to know what the things (electric switches) were on the wall.

York tried to explain what they did by relating electricity to water flowing in a stream.

Then he wanted to know why there were people with different skin colors now, since he had known of only one color when he lived. He also was interested in why we were going to the moon, since he had been there and found nothing on it.

York answered his questions and then asked him if there were other spirits with him.

William said he was completely alone.

York told him that other spirits were around, possibly in other planes, and William could contact them by willing himself to be with them.

York brought the lady out from under hypnosis and several days later she was told by William that he had found other spirits and would no longer come to her.

York's research seems fantastic to be coming from the Space Capital of the Universe where the moon vehicles originated, but more and more scientists are becoming convinced that the psychic realm should be investigated and understood.

Apparently the discarnate spirit, William, had spent thousands of years in the spirit world before he made contact with other spirits. He probably had a low sense of awareness in the psychic world, and therefore was unaware of any beings in the spirit world until York suggested that he try to contact other beings.

Unanswered Natural Universal Laws

In the same way that religionists assume that God or an intelligence is everywhere the same throughout the universe, the scientist assumes that the natural laws are the same throughout the entire physical universe. Where the scientist has been able to observe natural laws at a great distance through telescopes, he has found that natural laws are the same, billions of light years away, as they are on earth.

For example, the law of gravity has been observed at great distances in the motion of stars and galaxies. This law of nature is the same in these distant stars as it is in our solar system. Since it is the same, there must be some connection between this part of the universe and another part.

We know of no connection that causes natural laws to be the same everywhere, but we shall assume that the connection is in the psychic universe.

Also, assuming that a super-intelligent being is the cause of the natural laws, physical material, and order which we observe in the universe, he would need some instantaneous signal to contact various parts of his vast estate. He would seem to require such communication based upon how the earth's communication has been developed by us to keep the earth society functioning. He would use this psychic signal to contact beings such as ourselves, anywhere in the universe, but where beings were not present and he wished to shift the location of a planet, produce a new sun, or more matter for any reason, he would need a method for moving objects.

Thus he would need something like P-K to move planets where intelligent beings were not available to move the planets with nuclear power or other propulsive forces. Energy intelligence may use P-K as the natural method of moving objects when other natural forces are not available for the job. The universal mind, assuming he controls the universe, must have either an instantaneous signal to anywhere, or he must be located throughout the universe, which may be exactly the same, since the end result would be the same.

What would this mean to us as part of the universal mind? We should have the ability to move objects with our minds when we communicate on the psychic channel. We should develop the ability to go anywhere, using levitation, teleportation, etc. We may have to develop this ability primarily as a group or society rather than individually, since most of our technological progress has been by group effort.

There are apparently isolated cases of people who move objects with their mind, but these are random, non-consistent occurrences which are not predictable or reliable.

If we shall collectively work on developing P-K after understanding what it is, we shall have a fantastically useful force for service to mankind and other beings of our universe. This is a long-range program, but there may be isolated cases which prove that P-K will work for us.

Bodily Ascension

Here are some predictions of what can happen if we master P-K by a good communication link with universal intelligence.

We shall not die a physical death. We can cure illness, physical damage to our bodies, and stop the aging progress. When our work is completed on earth, we can proceed to our next assignment with our physical bodies intact, while communicating with all intelligent beings in the universe. We can leave the earth in the same manner that Elijah, Moses, Jesus, and many others have departed. Fantastic, but possible according to Jesus, who said that we could do even greater things than he did.

If we can prevent aging, why would we want to leave the earth?

We may want to leave for both negative and positive reasons. One negative reason for leaving is that we would not fit into the earth social system if we had psychic powers, like Jesus. We would be out of place with people because our relatives and others who are our lifetime friends would be dying. We would not fit into the legal systems for owning property, drawing social security, and other items associated with older people. We would not fit into the family system of being a grandparent, great grandparent, great great grandparent, etc., because our descendants wouldn't know what to do with us or how to explain such an unusual old fogey who just won't die.

On the positive side of reasons for leaving the earth, we would probably like to see other places and beings in the universe. We may want to go to where our deceased relatives are and visit with them. Our strongest motivation for moving on may be the desire to learn more about the physical and psychic universe.

If we use P-K and other psychic powers in this life, we can be an oddity who may even become unwelcome in society as was so vividly demonstrated in the life of Christ. We would either have to be very cautious in how and when we exercised our psychic power or accept a position in society as an outsider, oddball, or showpiece.

When we decide to leave earth, if we have mastered the ascension, we can rise through the air into a vehicle waiting to take us to our next assignment in the universe, or we can leave our bodies behind and pass into the spiritual universe where we shall be everywhere.

We can rematerialize a body at another location in the universe where we are assigned to continue our education. There is also the possibility that a future responsibility may require that we be born again as a child to work among some race on some primitive planet in the universe.

Anthony Brooke writing in *Fate* reports that Annalee Skarin mysteriously disappeared from Salt Lake City, Utah, in June, 1952. The circumstances surrounding her "translation" or "ascension" indicate that she had reached an ultimate in psycho-kinetic control of her physical body.

At one time a member of the Mormon Church, the publication of her book, *Ye Are Gods,* led to much conflict with the leaders of the church who claimed that she was setting herself up as a prophetess, a position reserved for the President of the Church of Jesus Christ of Latter-Day Saints. The dispute finally resulted in Mrs. Skarin being excommunicated.

Mrs. Skarin said, "All I am trying to do is teach mankind that it is possible for every child of God to be so in tune with Him and His Holy Spirit that they can be directed in all that they do, in all that they say, and that their lives can become a melody of living glory as they learn to abide completely and fully in His Holy Spirit. It is such a breathtaking glory every moment of every day that it is almost unspeakable in its power."

The alleged "translation" took place in the home of an elderly couple in June, 1952. Neither of these people feel that they have any reason to doubt the reality of the translation. They simply and readily accept it as a fact.

On the eventful morning of June 16, 1952, Mrs. Skarin hinted to her friend that she had been told the previous night that the angels might be coming for her soon. As a result, she gave orders that if this should happen, her daughter was to be sent all of her books and other personal effects.

In the early morning hours of June 17, Mrs. Skarin's friend wakened suddenly and felt compelled to go to Mrs. Skarin's room. She was gone! Nothing in the way of clothes or other belongings seemed to be missing. Even her dentures were laying on a bedside table. There was, however, a strange, light aroma that filled not only the room but the entire house. Mrs. Skarin's friend assumed that this aroma was what had awakened her so suddenly.

Late that same evening, while this friend and her grown son and two daughters were seated in the living room, Mrs. Skarin entered the house. She was wearing a plain blue dress, her hair was disheveled, and her legs were dusty.

Mrs. Skarin asked, "Do you believe I have translated?"

When those assembled there assured her that they did, Mrs. Skarin praised God for their faith and asked his blessing upon them.

Immediately, her appearance changed into a shining being clothed in white raiment; her hair shown with a golden light. One note of interest was the shining new teeth which Mrs. Skarin displayed, even though her dentures were laying on her bedside table upstairs.

Annalee continued to bless them as she slowly disappeared from their sight.

Annalee stated in her writings that man has embryonic divinity within himself. Every minute brain cell of man's being can become spiritualized and controlled by his mind. Further, she held that the experience of translation is not just for the few. It is intended for all. Yet, she insisted, we should not have our minds fixed on translation but on unceasing prayer, praise, and thanksgiving to God, which if intensively engaged in, must lead to this result.

Apparently Annalee had followed techniques established by universal energy intelligence, which to her provided such a close contact with him that she could have unlimited power, even to psycho-kinetically changing her body and transforming it into the psychic universe.

Her appearance of "shining" and hair that "shown with a golden light," indicated that her body was being converted into the materials around her–i.e. air, dust, etc.–and the psychical signal which performed this psycho-kinetic feat was releasing light. Then she disappeared because her physical body had transmuted, but Annalee was in the psychic universe. She had translated from a point in the physical universe to being spread everywhere in the psychic universe. Then she could again be born on another planet.

Overseers of Other Planets

This rebirth would not be a re-incarnation but a continuation of our spiritual selves in the psychic universe while a body develops in a normal biological manner on the assigned planet. The rebirth would be a linking up of the new physical brain with the spiritual soul in the unobstructed universe. We would be living in the physical universe with a communication to the psychic universe. This complete being would be one like Jesus.

It is also possible that no rebirth would be required, as we work on a planet or planets of the universe to help life develop from simple micro-organisms to Homo sapiens type beings.

Whether we already have, or produce, a physical body using P-K or exist only in the psychic universe seems unimportant for an overseer's job, until we make direct contact with beings at the Homo sapiens level. We would need a physical body which looked like the natives' bodies, so they would not be frightened. Then we could talk to them face to face, educating and encouraging them to develop their sixth sense for better communication with us.

The natives of our planet may think of us as angels or gods which we would be to them, but we would think of the natives as our children, because we would have used P-K to produce the changes in one species of life so that a new species evolved, until unintelligent life was at a level which would support a Homo sapiens level. This level would be the sub-human level, which is known to have existed thousands of years before God created Adam. The natives, our children, would be our primary joy and sorrow when they were at the Homo sapiens level, because they could communicate slightly with us, but would often make serious mistakes causing wars, sickness, and much distress for themselves and us because we loved them.

We, as overseers and parents, would have the responsibility of protecting our children as required, continuing to develop their awareness that a higher intelligence is available to help them. We would primarily be responsible for teaching our children the universal concept of love, which is vital before they could communicate in the psychic world and have the tremendous powers available there.

Love is a concern for the welfare of others. Love is a feeling we have toward another which is like the feeling we have for ourselves. Love is our desire for the happiness of other persons. Love is essential to our existence in the psychic realm and use of its powers, because in the unobstructed universe we are one with all spiritual beings, working together for common goals. As spirit beings we must lose ourselves, or we could use psychic powers to destroy parts of ourselves which would cause sorrow to ourselves.

"If I speak in the tongues of men and of angels, but have not love, I am a noisy gong or a clanging cymbal. And if I have prophetic powers, and understand all mysteries and all knowledge, and if I have all faith, so as to remove mountains, but have not love, I am nothing. If I give away all I have, and if I deliver my body to be burned but have not love, I gain nothing.

"Love is patient and kind; love is not jealous or boastful; it is not arrogant or rude. Love does not insist on its own way; it is not irritable or resentful; it does not rejoice at wrong, but rejoices in the right. Love bears all things, believes all things, hopes all things, endures all things.

"Love never ends; as for prophecies, they will pass away; as for tongues, they will cease; as for knowledge, it will pass away. For our knowledge is imperfect and our prophecy is imperfect; but when the perfect comes, the imperfect will pass away. When I was a child, I spoke like a child, I thought like a child, I reasoned like a child; when I became a man, I gave up childish ways. For now we see in a mirror dimly, but then face to face. Now I know in part; then I shall understand fully, even as I have been fully understood. So faith, hope, love abide, these three; but the greatest of these is love." *(I Corinthians 13 RSV)*

Probably the best way of teaching our children on our planet the true nature of love and how to live in the spirit realm is for us to live among our children for a while, practicing complete love as we have learned from our education in the unobstructed universe. This way was used by Jesus on earth 2,000 years ago. It is difficult for the majority of people today to understand the Jesus love, and it is much more difficult to practice it, because we have not developed a sufficiently good psychic communication link with Jesus to be aware, continually, of the best way to treat our fellowman.

It seems that the primary and ultimate goal of the existence of universal intelligence is to preserve intelligent beings in the universe. And to preserve intelligence, it may be necessary for additional knowledge to be obtained of how to stay alive, or exist, through some great cataclysm which may be coming as a natural function of the universe. This great cataclysm could be the collapse of the physical universe into one tremendous fireball of primary radiation particles, which destroys all physical material except energy, and may destroy the identity of spirit beings. If this were the case, the universal energy intelligence may be working on a plan to preserve himself.

Purpose of Biological Life on New Planets

Assuming new ideas are needed to preserve universal life, the purpose of beings like Homo sapiens on planets may be to develop new techniques for solving problems. Our purpose for existing with very little influence and help from the energy intelligence could be to allow us freedom for original thought. Techniques for solving problems on earth can then be applied to solving bigger problems in the physical universe when we become a part of universal life.

Another purpose for biological life of our level may be to convert matter into knowledge in the spirit universe which can be recycled back into matter in the physical world, thus continuing the cycle of life as long as the physical universe exists in its present form.

As a human beings eats food, he is converting some of the food directly into knowledge which is stored in the unobstructed universe. The human actually stores his knowledge in his brain but he also produces an electro-magnetic signal (light) which seems to be the link into the unobstructed universe, thus his knowledge becomes a part of the universal storage of knowledge. This stored knowledge can be used to solve universal problems or it can be recycled into the physical universe to produce matter and continue the physical universal cycle.

The cycle is: the changing of matter into chemical energy in the body of a human type being; the energy producing knowledge; the knowledge passing into the psychic realm where it is the unknown psychic material; the psychic material being converted back into light in the physical world; the light changing back into matter by pair production of an electron and a positron; the primary matter particles combining to form elements in stars; the stars producing planets where molecules are built up until some are complicated enough to be alive; then continued evolvement to higher forms of life with the help of universal life, until the Homo sapiens level is reached, where we can convert matter into knowledge in the psychic realm—thus completing the universal cycle, with biological life a vital link in the cycle. This cycle seems to be going on as the entire physical universe goes through its expansion, contraction, fireball, and expansion cycle. Many physical universe cycles may have occurred before any type of intelligence was able to exist through the fireball phase; however this may be the first cycle for intelligence.

In either case, the big project ahead of the universal energy intelligence may be how to maintain complete identity; i.e., not be destroyed as an intelligent being when the physical universe becomes a plasma of energy and primary basic sub-nuclear particles.

With such a tremendous vital goal in mind, we, as overseers of new biological life-support planets, would try to utilize any ideas or methods originating from the natives on the planets to devise a method for maintaining our identity through the universal fireball holocaust.

One possible way to prevent the holocaust, thus maintaining identity, may be using P-K to push the stars and galaxies apart, preventing collisions as the entire physical universe tries to converge at one point. This method may require a tremendous universal army of highly skilled P-K controllers, with immeasurable years of experience in using P-K throughout the vast universe.

To prevent the holocaust may be the ultimate in P-K use, but such a concept is only mental entertainment for those of us who have moved nothing with our minds linked up to energy intelligence.

At this time, the reader (if he has not already done so) should make an objective, critical analysis of himself. Ask yourself the questions: Do I want to have P-K powers? Am I convinced that such natural laws exist which will allow me to move objects with just thoughts? What actual attempts have I made to move even one object? What success have I had? Didn't I at least receive some message when I seriously attempted to move the object? Have I tried using P-K for some worthwhile purpose, such as healing a sick person or moving a seriously ill person to the hospital?

We should watch for occasions when there is a real need for P-K, then try to exercise it. Use P-K as a powerful force to make people happy.

In my field of science and engineering, there are many well-informed engineers and scientists who would not entertain the possibility that the unusual stories told in this book could be the result of natural laws not as yet understood. These men have closed minds. But there are also many professionals who have open minds and feel that many unusual occurrences are real events which have a natural explanation. Some of the more open-minded scientists are so convinced that psychic phenomena are natural that they are investigating these phenomena, while a few are actually trying to use psychic powers to communicate with the universal intelligence to learn more about the science of the occult. In my field of science, I am making progress in the understanding and use of spirit forces from the unobstructed universe, but have I mastered the control of psychic forces to move this pencil to write this book instead of moving the pencil with my mind?

Do I actually believe that I have proposed methods to develop use of P-K for the readers, or am I just trying to put down enough convincing words to sell books? If these methods of developing P-K control are any good, why am I not world-famous from using these powers on TV and the stage?

I can give very rational, convincing answers to all of these self-analysis questions, but are the answers satisfactory to others?

You may still think, "You talk a good line, but let's see just one small object lift off a table and float across the room! Produce, and I'll be convinced!"

But let's re-examine what I have said. I have not claimed that I move objects with my mind for purposes of convincing others that it's possible. I have suggested that each person should attempt to use his mind to perform useful acts of P-K and let others know the results. If others hear about feats of P-K, they will overcome their skepticism and also try to find out more about this strange power and its source.

As more and more people are aware of the psychic universe and the forces available there, we shall have more and more success in psychic controls. We may have to work together as we do in many big projects to gain effective use of P-K and other spiritual powers.

We can improve our sixth sense if we are convinced that we have a sixth sense which can communicate with the universal energy intelligence. We shall find that all attempts to communicate with him are rewarded by a response from him.

In each opportunity that we have to help another person, as we express love by aiding him, we help our sixth sense develop. To become greatest in the psychic universe is to be one who is a servant of others. We cannot express love to another unless we perform physical services. We cannot perform physical services unless we have personal contact. To say that we love a person but will not associate with him is paradoxical. Those we love we are with and helping.

As our love grows our service to others grows, and our ability to control P-K and other psychic forces will increase.